ROSSETTI AND HIS CIRCLE

ROSSETTI AND HIS CIRCLE

Elizabeth Prettejohn

Stewart, Tabori & Chang
New York

Acknowledgments

I am grateful to Charles Martindale, Christopher Newall, Richard Humphreys, and Simon Wilson for their comments on the manuscript; Judith Severne has been a sympathetic and expert editor. I owe a great debt to Alastair Grieve for his writing and thought on Rossetti. Griselda Pollock's work is the major influence on my treatment of issues about the female figure.

Elizabeth Prettejohn

© 1997 Elizabeth Prettejohn. All Rights Reserved.

Designed by Herman Lelie
Typeset by Stefania Bonelli

Published by order of the Trustees of the Tate Gallery
by Tate Gallery Publishing, Millbank, London SW1P 4RG

Published in 1998 and distributed in the U.S. by
Stewart, Tabori & Chang,
a division of U.S. Media Holdings, Inc.
115 West 18th Street, New York, NY 10011

Distributed in Canada b General Publishing Co., Ltd.
30 Lesmill Road, Don Mills, Ontario, Canada M3B 2T6

Library of Congress Catalog Card Number: TK 97-65596

ISBN: 1-55670-656-1

Printed in Great Britain by Balding + Mansell, Norwich, England
10 9 8 7 6 5 4 3 2 1

Front cover: D.G. Rossetti, *Lady Lileth* 1864–8 (detail of fig.24)
Back cover: Edward Burne-Jones, *The Golden Stairs* 1880 (fig.52)
Frontispiece: Albert Moore, *Azaleas* exh.1868 (detail of fig.35)

CONTENTS

INTRODUCTION: BEYOND PRE-RAPHAELITISM

Most of the art we call Pre-Raphaelite has nothing to do with the Pre-Raphaelite Brotherhood. The richly coloured paintings of sensual women by Dante Gabriel Rossetti, Edward Burne-Jones, John William Waterhouse, and others are irresistible to the publishers of coffee-table books, calendars, posters, and greetings cards; these images have become the most familiar works popularly called 'Pre-Raphaelite'. But of their painters only Rossetti himself was ever a member of the Pre-Raphaelite Brotherhood, and the images date from a later period than the Pre-Raphaelite heyday, from 1848 to about 1853.

The familiar pictures of women relate to a different social context: the circle of artists who clustered around Rossetti after his move in 1862 to Tudor House, beside the Thames in Chelsea. That circle has its own glamour: the group's Bohemian lifestyle, with its hints of scandal, attracted gossip from the first, and can still seem romantically shocking more than a century later. But its members – including Burne-Jones, William Morris, James McNeill Whistler, and the poet Algernon Charles Swinburne – had no connection to the original Pre-Raphaelite Brotherhood, except through Rossetti. One reason for using the label 'Pre-Raphaelite' is simply convenience; the more informal later grouping never adopted a name or slogan. Another reason may be less innocuous. Modern publishers trade on the pictures' eroticism, but they disguise it as art history under the respectable term, Pre-Raphaelitism.

To call Rossetti's later circle Pre-Raphaelite is to obscure its distinctive identity. The eroticism and luscious handling of the pictures of women, so different from the moralising subjects and meticulous technique of the Pre-Raphaelite Brotherhood, mark not just a new type of picture, but a new conception of art's impact on the viewer. The change might be described as a shift away from Pre-Raphaelite realism; no

longer was the emphasis on objective description of the external world. The pictures claimed to offer not information to be filtered through the intellect, but direct experience for the senses, powerful in its immediacy. Eroticism was only the most obvious aspect of that experience.

In the last decades of the nineteenth century, the art of Rossetti's circle made a profound impression in France and elsewhere on the Continent. It became a crucial point of reference for continental writers and artists who were themselves moving away from realism, toward what was christened Symbolism in 1886. For the continental Symbolists, and for the *fin-de-siècle* generation in Britain, the pictures of Rossetti and his associates suggested spiritual and symbolic resonances that could not be explained in realist terms. The haunting faces of women, the profusion of sumptuous flowers, the exotic settings seemed to lead the imagination far beyond prosaic modern reality toward deeper meanings, ancient memories, forgotten worlds. The poet W.B. Yeats compared the painting of Rossetti and Whistler to Wagner's music and to the poetry of Keats and Verlaine. Such art, he wrote, had 'accepted all symbolisms, the symbolism of the ancient shepherds and star-gazers, that symbolism of bodily beauty which seemed a wicked thing to Fra Angelico, the symbolism in day and night, and winter and summer, spring and autumn'. Yeats's description weaves together the immediate sensuous impact of the art with suggestions of mysticism and spirituality.

Whether interpreted as erotic or spiritual, the art of Rossetti's circle has been a constant source of fascination – for its original Victorian audiences and for the continental Symbolists, as well as the modern consumers of calendar and poster art. This book will explore the origins and dimensions of that fascination in the distinctive artistic milieu of Rossetti's social circle.

fig.1 D.G. Rossetti **Veronica Veronese** 1872, oil on canvas 109.2 × 88.8 cm
Delaware Art Museum, Samuel and Mary R. Bancroft Memorial Collection

DANTE GABRIEL ROSSETTI

Symbolising the Artist: Dante Gabriel Rossetti

As both a painter and a poet, Rossetti (1828-82) has attracted the attentions of numerous biographers. And indeed the events of his life lend themselves readily to glamorisation, even though the artist rarely ventured far from home and played no role in Victorian public life. He was the son of an exiled Italian patriot and Dante scholar. Hence his name, Gabriel Charles Dante Rossetti at his christening, then altered to its familiar form, more succinctly romantic: Dante, for the medieval poet; Gabriel, hinting at the angel of the Annunciation; Rossetti, the Italian surname that sounded strange in Victorian England. Other Rossettis also excite the imagination; not only the father, with his abstruse studies of Dante, but the brother William Michael, political radical, agnostic, and devotee of Shelley, and the sister Christina Georgina (fig.2), the devout poet who never married, but lived out an ideal of dedication to art and religion no less intriguing than the life of her artist brother.

Dante Gabriel Rossetti's early career conformed to the romantic stereotype of the precocious genius; he composed his most famous poem, 'The Blessed Damozel', before the age of nineteen. His pencil self-portrait (fig.3), from about that time, suggests that he was already projecting a persona as youthful romantic genius, like the young Keats or Shelley: his face is boyishly smooth, with a white highlight on the prominent forehead suggesting a powerful intellect, full lips hinting at the sensual, and shoulder-length wavy locks just disorderly enough to intimate the genius's carelessness about conventional proprieties. Just over a year later, in 1848, he helped to found the most famous of English artistic movements, the Pre-Raphaelite Brotherhood, playing out another myth of the artist's life – that of youthful solidarity with other creative spirits. In later years, there was fierce debate about which of the young artists was the prime mover in the Brotherhood: William Holman Hunt, John Everett Millais, or Rossetti himself. That question is irresolvable, but the debates helped to keep alive the fame of the Brotherhood, long after the first blaze of publicity had receded into history.

We may never know just how controversial the Brotherhood really was, when it burst on the London art world in 1849 and 1850 – later writers have perhaps overemphasised

fig.2 D.G. Rossetti **Christina Georgina Rossetti and her Mother, Frances Mary Lavinia Rossetti** 1877
crayon on paper 42.2 × 48.3 cm, National Portrait Gallery

fig.3 D.G. Rossetti **Self-Portrait** March 1847
pencil heightened with white on paper 19.1 × 19.7 cm
National Portrait Gallery

public hostility to the Pre-Raphaelites, in order to bolster the artists' reputations as misunderstood geniuses. But it may have been, as the Rossetti legend has it, that harsh reviews of the first paintings of the Brotherhood caused Rossetti to retreat permanently from the world of public exhibition. He rarely exhibited in public after 1850, instead allowing curiosity to gather around his image as the mysterious painter whose work was perpetually invisible.

So Rossetti's life on the public stage virtually ceased when he was just twenty-two. Nonetheless, his subsequent private life offers more than sufficient incident for biographers. The death in 1862 of his wife Elizabeth Siddall, from an overdose of laudanum, was apparently a suicide but the precise causes remain mysterious. The exhumation of Siddall's body in 1869, to retrieve the manuscript volume of Rossetti's poems that had been twined in her hair at her burial, adds a touch of the macabre to the life story. Rossetti's romantic obsession with the wife of another famous man, William Morris, resulted in a series of paintings of the woman, born Jane Burden, so mannered as to enrapture some viewers and repel others (figs.6, 57). His nervous breakdown of 1872 has been variously attributed to the failure of his love affair with Jane Burden Morris, to a paranoid reaction to harsh press criticism of his 1870 volume of poetry, and to drug addiction – any of these causes perfectly conformable with the romantic notion of the tortured creative artist. So too his subsequent withdrawal from society and rapidly declining health, leading to his death just before his fifty-fourth birthday.

Rossetti's life, then, is itself a legend. Its events, as biographers have immortalised them, have become a series of symbols of the creative artist: the adolescent prodigy, the young rebel, the misunderstood genius, the reclusive creator, the passionate lover, the drug-dependent visionary, the expressionist madman. For these mythical phases, Rossetti's compelling paintings have come to stand as material evidence. Intensity of colour combined with erratic draughtsmanship, along with the obsessive repetition of a few compositional types – these are all too easy to romanticise

fig.4 D.G. Rossetti **Beata Beatrix** c.1864–70 oil on canvas 86.4 × 66 cm, Tate Gallery

as signs of the madness of genius, as in the case of a near-contemporary, Vincent van Gogh. Indeed, it is difficult to decide whether the paintings symbolise the life of the artist, or whether biographers have dramatised the events of the life as symbols for the paintings.

Nowhere is this more apparent than in the succession of images representing the women in Rossetti's life. Rossetti's biographers have used the images of the different women as talismans, each woman symbolising a different phase in the artist's spiritual development. In most accounts, Rossetti's fiancée and wife Elizabeth Siddall functions as the sign of the artist's youthful idealism. In *Beata Beatrix* (fig.4), she appears as a conflation of herself and Dante's Beatrice, the most celebrated symbol of spiritualised love in the history of Western literature, and one with special resonances for the Italian poet's nineteenth-century namesake. The female figure appears trancelike, already half-departed from the earthly world, while a red bird offers her a poppy, emblem of death; the personified figure of Love, on the left, complements the figure of Dante on the right, both dim in the picture's muted colouring.

In dramatic contrast is Fanny Cornforth, the woman of dubious reputation, perhaps even a prostitute, who enters Rossetti's life in the later 1850s; images of Cornforth are taken to epitomise Rossetti's development of the sensual side of his nature – and his art. In the *Blue Bower* (fig.5) there is no scholarly reference to a literary source, only a languid woman dressed in furs and jewels, and playing a dulcimer to evoke the sensory pleasures of music; the robust physical type is utterly different from Siddall's wan delicacy.

fig.5 D.G. Rossetti **The Blue Bower** 1865
oil on canvas 82.6 × 69.2 cm
Barber Institute of Fine Arts, The University of Birmingham

Siddall and Cornforth, then, appear as dialectical opposites, respectively symbolising the spiritual and the physical, the soul and the body. As wife and mistress, they easily come to stand for virtue and vice. Finally, toward the later 1860s, Jane Burden Morris begins to appear in Rossetti's art; she is often taken to reconcile the opposites, to unite the spiritual with the sensuous, to heal the rupture in Rossetti's nature. In *Proserpine* (fig.6), she takes the role of the mythological goddess who mediated between life and death, spending half the year in the underworld with her husband Pluto, the other half in eternally renewed life on earth.

So the images of women can be organised into a neat tripartite scheme: Siddall versus Cornforth, with Burden as synthesis. In this scheme, the women lose their own identities to become mere signs of different aspects of Rossetti's identity. The artist develops the spiritual and sensuous sides of his art separately; as he reaches creative maturity he synthesises the contrasting sides of his genius into a coherent aesthetic whole. It is scarcely surprising that this tripartite biographical scheme, for Rossetti, corresponds to a tripartite scheme for art in general, common in nineteenth-century art theory: the spiritual aspect of art was pitted against its sensuous aspect, but many theorists argued that the greatest art was that which united those two poles.

To see Rossetti's images of different women as symbolising the phases of his artistic development is only one interpretation for the pictures, one that has been prevalent in biographically oriented studies of the artist, but by no means the only possibility. Rossetti's pictures were not ordinarily exhibited in public; nonetheless, their significance is not limited to Rossetti's private life – they are not merely autobiographical footprints. To explore some of the other meanings of the pictures, it is necessary to step back and place Rossetti's art in perspective, as part of the world in which he lived and worked.

fig.6 D.G. Rossetti **Proserpine** 1877
oil on canvas 125.1 × 61 cm
Tate Gallery

Pre-Raphaelitism and its Symbolism

The Pre-Raphaelite Brotherhood has been celebrated both as a realist movement, dedicated singlemindedly to an ideal of truth-to-nature, and as a revivalist movement, drawing inspiration from the art of the period before Raphael. The two interpretations are not incompatible. The Pre-Raphaelites shared the growing enthusiasm of their Victorian contemporaries for what seemed the freshness of the early Renaissance artists' response to the natural world; they believed that later art had increased in technical sophistication only to lose the direct response to nature of the earlier artists. To emulate the spirit of early Renaissance art was, on this view, to be a realist.

Such aims may be traced in Rossetti's first Pre-Raphaelite painting, indeed the first oil painting the young artist brought to completion, *The Girlhood of Mary Virgin* (fig.7), exhibited in 1849. The lily, standing in a vase atop a pile of books before the seated Virgin, serves two functions simultaneously. It is the model for the lily in the young Virgin's embroidery. Indeed, the Virgin herself appears as a realist artist, scrupulously copying nature in her embroidery silks. However, the lily is also a traditional symbol for the Virgin Mary's purity or innocence, indeed the most familiar symbol for the Virgin in Renaissance painting. Rossetti's lily, then, encapsulates both aspects of the Pre-Raphaelite project, truth-to-nature and the inspiration of early Renaissance painting.

The Pre-Raphaelite notion of realism meant that each configuration of coloured marks, on the canvas, stood for one particular object in the real world – not just any flower dashed off in a scumble of pigment, but a particular lily with its petals and leaves precisely delineated. In analogous fashion, Pre-Raphaelite symbolism meant that each visible symbol stood for one particular symbolised concept, as the lily stood for innocence. The lily is only one of a multitude of symbols in the picture, each of which can be decoded to arrive at its particular meaning. To assist viewers in the decoding process, Rossetti wrote a pair of explanatory sonnets, one inscribed on the original picture frame, the other printed in the exhibition catalogue. The first line of the second sonnet announces that it is the key to the code: 'These are the symbols'. The sonnet goes on to explain:

> The books (whose head
> Is golden Charity, as Paul hath said)
> Those virtues are wherein the soul is rich:
> Therefore on them the lily standeth, which
> Is Innocence, being interpreted.
> The seven-thorned briar and the palm
> seven-leaved
> Are her great sorrows and her great reward.

The sonnet specifies a one-to-one correspondence between each symbol and its symbolised concept: books for virtues, lily for innocence, briar for sorrows, palm for reward. With a little knowledge, and a great deal of patience, the spectator can decode each symbol to gain a wealth of information about the Virgin, her life, education, and virtuous character.

Pre-Raphaelite technique was admirably suited to this painstaking method of symbolism. Rossetti's friend, the painter and poet William Bell Scott, observed him working on *The Girlhood of Mary Virgin* with small watercolour brushes, even though he was painting in oils. The resulting small-scale touch permits each symbolic element to stand out clearly, down to minute details such as the lettering on the spines of the books. Scott also noted that Rossetti applied his paint thinly, on a surface which had previously been primed with a smooth white ground. That preparation gave the colours, when they were laid on top, a special brilliancy. Again this technique related simultaneously to both aspects of the Pre-Raphaelite programme. It mimicked the light, pure colour of early Renaissance fresco painting, rather than the richer and moodier tonalities of later oil painting. At the same time, it permitted sharp colour contrasts that assisted the realist project of describing each particular object.

D.G. Rossetti **The Girlhood of Mary Virgin** 1848–9
(detail of fig.7)

The Pre-Raphaelite approach to symbolism was exacting. Each symbol had clearly to demonstrate its one-to-one correspondence to the concept it symbolised; at the same time, each had to be plausible as a realistic element in the situation represented. *The Girlhood of Mary Virgin* shows the young Rossetti taking utmost pains to conform to this rigorous method, but his allegiance was short-lived. 'Of such direct aids to expression Rossetti soon took leave', wrote Frederic George Stephens, the Pre-Raphaelite Brother who subsequently became an influential art critic. Rossetti would fill his later works with what Stephens called 'more recondite emblems', still essential to the pictures' impact, but no longer amenable to one-to-one decoding.

fig.7 D.G. Rossetti **The Girlhood of Mary Virgin** 1948–9
oil on canvas 83.2 × 65.4 cm, Tate Gallery

Bocca Baciata

In the 1850s the Pre-Raphaelite Brothers drifted apart, both socially and artistically; Rossetti withdrew from the realm of public exhibition to concentrate on small-scale works in watercolour. In 1859 he suddenly returned to oil painting, but the technique he now adopted was markedly different from that of *The Girlhood of Mary Virgin*. The picture eventually known as *Bocca Baciata* (fig.8) was painted in opulent, glowing colours that produce a strong sense of the physicality of the paint, allied to a new physical immediacy in the close-up presentation of the single female figure. Both the technique and the compositional formula relate to a growing interest in Venetian painting among Rossetti's contemporaries. The sumptuous colour, robust figure types, and opulent settings of Venetian paintings, such as those of Titian and Giorgione, were celebrated for their direct impact on the viewer's senses, in abrupt opposition to the religious austerity and intellectual rigour ascribed to the early Renaissance art of Florence and Rome.

With the change in technique came a different approach to the subject matter and symbolism – 'recondite' indeed, in comparison to the straightforward symbolism of *The Girlhood of Mary Virgin*. Who is this anonymous woman? The rose in her hair seems straightforward enough, a traditional symbol of love. But why is she holding a marigold, often used as a symbol of grief, here repeated as the main motif of the background? What is the bizarre ornament in her luxuriant red hair? And why is there an apple on the ledge before her? The apple might be that of the Garden of Eden, symbolising sexual temptation; it might be the attribute of the pagan goddess Venus, signifying love or beauty; or it might be a simpler but equally traditional visual analogue for a woman's breast – the real woman's breast is next to it, although hidden under her bodice.

The combination of the 'Venetian' painting technique with the presentation of the figure, hair unbound and bodice unbuttoned, coalesces around a theme or mood of sensuality, confirmed by the title. The phrase *Bocca Baciata* is

fig.8 D.G. Rossetti **Bocca Baciata** 1859
oil on panel 32.1 × 27 cm
Museum of Fine Arts, Boston. Gift of James Lawrence

aster – a daring message indeed for England in 1859. It was perhaps to mute that implication that F.G. Stephens later described the marigolds as emblems of bereavement; the woman might then be a poignantly youthful, but perfectly respectable widow. The visual signs in the picture can support any of these readings: female sexuality as danger, promiscuity as bliss, or female beauty as poignant in adversity.

Another approach is to suggest a purely private interpretation, along the lines explored above. The model for the figure was Fanny Cornforth, the woman who excited in Rossetti a more carnal desire than the love he felt for Siddall. Moreover, she apparently conferred her sexual favours also on the man who commissioned the picture, Rossetti's painter-friend George Price Boyce. While the picture was being planned, Rossetti referred to it simply as a portrait; it might be seen, then, as an attempt to capture Cornforth's sensuality on canvas. The line from Boccaccio, appended later, might be a private joke between the two men, an agreement that they could both enjoy Cornforth's kisses.

But the picture is not merely a document of the unorthodox sexual triangle among Cornforth, Rossetti, and Boyce; it shares too much with other pictures of its time to be limited to a purely private interpretation. At the Royal Academy exhibition of 1859, just before *Bocca Baciata* was begun, were three paintings of a striking Italian model by Frederic Leighton, an artist two years younger than Rossetti who mixed in similar artistic circles. Leighton's pictures also deprived the female figure of a decodable narrative and symbolic context, annotating her beauty instead with attributes whose symbolism is vague or confusing. *Pavonia* (fig.9), for instance, takes its title from the Italian word for peacock, and skilfully sets the figure's sleek black hair in relief against a peacock-feather fan, compositionally analogous to Rossetti's marigolds. Perhaps the peacock feathers stand for the sumptuous visual display of the peacock's tail, transferred to this display of the woman's physical beauty. The peacock can also symbolise immortality or watchfulness, through the multiple 'eyes' of the tail; it is a traditional attribute of the goddess Juno, perhaps hinting at queenliness for the

excerpted from a line in the Decameron, by the fourteenth-century Italian writer Giovanni Boccaccio: 'the mouth that has been kissed does not lose its savour, indeed it renews itself just as the moon does'. The symbolic elements fit that theme well enough – even the strange hair ornament adds to the woman's sensual allure. But the various symbols point to a generalised mood rather than particular concepts; attempts to give them one-to-one readings fail to yield an unambiguous message. The American scholar Sarah Phelps Smith ingeniously suggests that the woman is a temptress (hence the apple), offering grief (the marigold) in return for the kiss of the title. But the full line from Boccaccio suggests that the promiscuous kiss may lead to bliss rather than dis-

woman. But the figure's social class and circumstances are unclear. Her gathered white bodice is of the type given to Italian peasant women in nineteenth-century painting, but the pearls and gleaming silk of her headdress indicate a higher social status. The way Leighton's figure turns in space is very different from the frontal presentation of the figure in *Bocca Baciata* but emphasises her sensuality in another way; the back of the chair in Leighton's picture functions like the parapet in Rossetti's to place a barrier between the desired woman and the desiring viewer. The gazes of both figures are intriguingly enigmatic; although Leighton's appears readier to solicit the viewer's attention, neither figure's eyes quite promise the woman's availability.

Rossetti's picture was not unique, then, in its tantalising presentation of a single female figure with luxurious, but puzzling, attributes. Nor was Rossetti's new interest in Venetian art unusual for the late 1850s; contemporary periodicals were devoting increasing attention to the Venetian High Renaissance, and the National Gallery had been acquiring major works of that period. But Rossetti's was not a balanced view; he gave extreme emphasis to the qualities seen as most sensual in Venetian painting, such as Titianesque red hair, opulence of colour, and figural corporeality. His former Pre-Raphaelite Brother, William Holman Hunt, responded with something like horror, describing the picture in a contemporary letter as 'remarkable for gross sensuality of a revolting kind'. Rossetti, he thought, was 'advocating as a principle mere gratification of the eye and if any passion at all – the animal passion to be the end of Art'. The difficulty of establishing an intellectually coherent meaning for the picture may have contributed to the distaste felt by Hunt, the most rigorous of the Pre-Raphaelites in his adherence to one-to-one symbolism.

What shocked Hunt proved fascinating to others – in particular, the young artists and writers who had entered Rossetti's orbit since the days of the Pre-Raphaelite Brotherhood. By the time *Bocca Baciata* was painted, Rossetti was close to Edward Burne-Jones, William Morris, and Algernon Charles Swinburne; those friendships had coalesced in 1857, when Rossetti had led an ambitious project to decorate the newly built Oxford Union Debating Chamber with mural paintings while the younger men were undergraduates. The murals deteriorated almost immediately due to technical problems, but the friendships persisted, with important results for the art of the next decades.

fig.9 Frederic Leighton **Pavonia** 1859
oil on canvas 53 × 41.5 cm
Private Collection

BOHEMIA IN LONDON

The Myth of Bohemia

> To be young, to be fond of pleasure, to care
> nothing for worldly prosperity, to scorn mere
> respectability, and to rebel against rigid rule, –
> these are the qualities which alone may be
> regarded as essential to constitute the Bohemian.
> *Westminster Review*, 1863

The lifestyle of Rossetti and his friends has often been called 'Bohemian' in a casual sense, referring to their mildly shocking behaviour. Rumours accumulated about the unconventional ménage at Tudor House in Cheyne Walk (fig.10), beside the Thames in Chelsea, where Rossetti's lodgers intermittently included his brother William Michael, the writers Swinburne and George Meredith, and the painter Frederick Sandys. There was gossip about Rossetti's love affairs; about Swinburne and the painter Simeon Solomon sliding naked down the bannisters; about nocturnal poetry readings and impromptu parties; about Rossetti angrily hurling a cup of scalding tea at Meredith, fortunately missing his aim; about Swinburne's drunkenness, and his failure to pay his rent. In a letter of 1865, Rossetti referred to Swinburne's impending return to Tudor House after a brief absence as 'a crisis not appreciably differing from a return of this house and neighbourhood to the primal elements of chaos'.

However, the painters and poets of the Rossetti circle can be called Bohemian in a more precise sense. Not only their lifestyle, but their art can be related to specific contemporary notions of Bohemianism, which attracted much discussion in England in the 1860s as articles on the subject began to appear in literary magazines. The word had originally been associated with the gipsies, popularly believed to have migrated from the central European kingdom of Bohemia. By analogy with the gipsies' refusal to integrate into modern industrial society, the word 'Bohemian' began to be used of French artists who declared their alienation from conventional society, particularly after the 'bourgeois' Revolution of 1830. That second sense of the word became current in England through the writings of the novelist William Makepeace Thackeray, who had lived in Paris as an art student in the 1830s.

Both notions of the Bohemian life are relevant to the Rossetti circle. Frederick Sandys spent time in gipsy encampments, forming a relationship with a gipsy woman called Keomi, who posed not only for Sandys but for the right-hand figure in Rossetti's *The Beloved* (fig.16); Meredith, too, introduced a gipsy character called Kiomi, evidently based on the same woman, into his novel of 1871, *The Adventures of Harry Richmond*. At the same time, members of Rossetti's circle were fascinated by French notions of the artist's 'Bohemian' independence from society. The young American artist James McNeill Whistler became close to the

fig.10 Tudor House, Cheyne Walk, Chelsea

fig.11 James McNeill Whistler **An Artist in his Studio** *c.*1856 pen and ink 23.4 cm diam., Freer Gallery of Art, Smithsonian Institution, Washington, D.C.

Rossetti circle in the summer of 1862, bringing with him tales of the art student's life he had lived in Paris in the later 1850s (fig.11). Through Whistler's contacts in Paris, Swinburne hoped to meet the French writers who flamboyantly declared art's independence from conventional moral norms, Charles Baudelaire and Théophile Gautier. Although those meetings never took place, Swinburne's enthusiasm for the French writers' works was crucial to the circle's evolving notions about art. Swinburne introduced even more flagrant French immorality to the circle; Boyce reported finding him and Rossetti poring over a copy of *Justine*, the notoriously licentious novel by the eighteenth-century French writer and pornographer, the Marquis de Sade, whose name was the origin for the term 'sadism'.

English writers continued to speak of artistic Bohemia as a distinctively Parisian phenomenon. The classic French novel of the Bohemian life, Henri Murger's *Scènes de la vie de*

Bohème of 1849, was extensively discussed in the English press from the 1860s onward, but not translated into English until 1887. Perhaps the financial irresponsibility and sexual exploits of its artist characters scared English publishers mindful of the conservative circulating libraries, the crucial market for literature in England. But that would have made the French notion of Bohemia all the more attractive, as a keynote of rebellion from conventional society, for the artists and writers of the Rossetti circle. The group centred on Tudor House developed a London version of the myth of artistic Bohemia, evident to some extent in their lives, even more so in their art.

The artists' district in early Victorian London was in and around Fitzroy Square, where the grandest house was inhabited by Sir Charles Eastlake, President of the Royal Academy from 1850 to 1865; the studio shared by Rossetti and Holman Hunt in the early days of the Pre-Raphaelite Brotherhood was nearby in Cleveland Street. A few artists, including J.M.W. Turner, had lived in Chelsea, away from the centre of the art world. Nonetheless, Rossetti's decision to move there was a declaration of independence from the mainstream (fig.12). One attraction was the possibility of living in a large house at a cheap rent; Chelsea was not then the expensive district it has subsequently become, partly due to its glamour as a haunt for artists following Rossetti's lead. Rossetti had contemplated the move even before the death of his wife Elizabeth Siddall, early in 1862. In the event Rossetti went alone to Tudor House, and that gave

fig.12 James McNeill Whistler **'The Adam and Eve' Old Chelsea** 1879 etching 17.3 × 29.9 cm, Art Gallery of Ontario, Toronto, Gift of Inco Limited, 1983

the distinctive tone to the project: the large, old-fashioned house became the focus of masculine artistic cameraderie, with a shifting assortment of temporary lodgers and informal visitors, unconstrained by the social conventions that the presence of middle-class women would have necessitated.

Burne-Jones, Morris, and Rossetti's old friend, Ford Madox Brown, were all married men; their wives were occasionally invited to visit, along with Rossetti's sisters and mother. But the day-to-day cast of characters at Tudor House was male and professionally dedicated to painting or writing; or female and involved in illicit liaisons with the men. Informal visiting was common between Rossetti and Fanny Cornforth, on the one hand, and Whistler and his mistress-model Joanna Hiffernan, on the other; Georgiana Burne-Jones and Jane Burden Morris did not mix with Cornforth and Hiffernan. The social pattern at Tudor House was not unlike that of Murger's *Scènes de la vie de Bohème*, but very unlike that of most London artists of the period.

A photograph of a gathering in the garden of Tudor House (fig.13), taken around 1863, shows Cornforth among a male confraternity that includes, from left to right, Swinburne, Rossetti, and William Michael Rossetti. This is almost a parody of a conventional Victorian family photograph, with Swinburne in the role of eccentric younger brother or nephew, and Cornforth enthroned in the position usually reserved for the mother. Rossetti presides over the party with an expansive gesture appropriate to paternal authority. But the only orthodox family relationship in the photograph is that between the brothers, Dante Gabriel and William Michael Rossetti.

fig.13 **Swinburne, D.G. Rossetti, Cornforth, and W.M. Rossetti in the garden at Tudor House** *c.*1863, probably by William Downey, albumen print, carte-de-visite size, Private Collection

New Approaches to Symbolism

A mania for collecting was one conspicuous feature of the Rossetti circle's lifestyle. Blue-and-white china, stray fragments of medieval armour, Venetian glass, exotic textiles, antiquated and probably unplayable musical instruments littered the artists' studios and reappeared in painted form, as accessories in pictures. In one sense this was nothing new; it was routine for earlier Victorian artists to accumulate collections of items for use as pictorial accessories. A painter who specialised in scenes from seventeenth-century English history, for instance, could be expected to own specimens of authentic Cavalier and Roundhead armour, ready to hand for copying into pictures.

However, in the Rossetti circle the collecting urge was more obsessive. Whistler and Rossetti competed, sometimes acrimoniously, for the Far Eastern ceramics they both collected. Rossetti even collected live animals, transforming his London garden into a menagerie; Boyce mentioned seeing a barn owl, peacocks, ravens, and a marmot at Tudor House, and the entire circle mourned the death of Rossetti's wombat in 1869. Rossetti's drawing of himself (fig.14), grief-stricken before the wombat's grave, satirises his own eccentricity.

fig.14 D.G. Rossetti, **Self-Portrait of the Artist Weeping at the Wombat's Tomb** 1869, pen, ink and brown wash on paper 17.9 × 11.3 cm, Trustees of the British Museum

But the collections of Rossetti and his friends differed in kind, as well as obsessiveness, from earlier artists' collections; the objects did not serve the utilitarian function of assuring historical accuracy in pictures. Indeed, the artists collected avidly in areas that had little or no relation to the subject matter of their pictures; they were among the earliest Western collectors of Japanese objects, available in Europe only after the opening of diplomatic relations with Japan in 1853. Japanese and Chinese objects appeared in the pictures alongside Western accessories of diverse provenances, with flagrant disregard for historical or geographical consistency. Rossetti's *The Beloved* (fig.16) ostensibly represented a biblical scene, showing the Bride of the Song of Solomon, surrounded by her hand-maidens. But the dress she wears is no accurate costume from the biblical Near East; instead, Rossetti borrowed a green Japanese robe from his friend Boyce, as well as an equally anachronistic jewelled ornament for the head of the black child. Burne-Jones's *Cinderella* of 1863 (fig.17) appears before a dresser filled with Chinese blue-and-white porcelain of the kind avidly collected by his friends, but bizarre in the context of the medieval fairy tale. Whistler's paintings and designs often combined Japanese fans and parasols with European figures in classicising draperies (fig.19).

These anachronistic or incongruous objects have usually been interpreted as purely decorative, inserted simply to add notes of vivid colour or because their shapes were visually pleasing. Nonetheless, their inclusion represented part of the Bohemian refusal to conform to conventional rules, in this case the generally accepted rule that all objects in a picture should be plausible as realistic elements in the represented time and place. Often the objects contradicted another basic convention of Victorian narrative painting, that the symbolic meanings of the accessories should help to elucidate the subject-matter. As seen above, each of the accessories in Rossetti's early picture, *The Girlhood of Mary Virgin*, symbolises a particular aspect of the picture's subject. But the Japanese dress and extravagant jewels in *The Beloved* do not relate so neatly to the subject matter. In a general sense, their gorgeousness elaborates the overall theme of the bride's physical

fig.16 D.G. Rossetti, **The Beloved ('The Bride')** 1865–6
oil on canvas 82.6 × 76.2 cm
Tate Gallery

fig.17 D.G. Rossetti **Helen of Troy** 1863
oil on panel, 32.8 × 27.7 cm
Hamburger Kunsthalle

fig.18 Frederick Sandys **Helen of Troy** *c.*1867
oil on panel 38.4 × 30.5 cm Board of Trustees of the National Museums
and Galleries on Merseyside (Walker Art Gallery, Liverpool)

beauty, but the objects can no longer be decoded individually.

This dissolution of the one-to-one tie between symbolic object and symbolised concept could lead in either of two directions. On the one hand, the object might fail to relate to any symbolised concept at all – becoming, paradoxically, a non-symbolising symbol. The hair ornaments in *The Beloved*, like the one in the earlier *Bocca Baciata*, are so conspicuous and elaborate that they compel the viewer to consider them as symbols, but it is difficult to say what concept they might symbolise. On the other hand, the symbolic object might suggest a number of concepts, rather than referring directly to one particular concept – becoming a proliferating symbol. The bride's hair ornament is opulent, so it might symbolise material wealth; it is positioned like a crown, so it might symbolise queenliness; it is coloured red, so it might symbolise passion; it is sharp-edged, so it might symbolise the danger of love or marriage. Again, the bride's green Japanese robe could be regarded as a non-symbolising symbol, because it is nonsensical in the biblical context of the subject matter. Or it might be interpreted as a proliferating symbol, leading the spectator's imagination to muse on some transcendent harmony between Eastern and Western ideals of beauty, or on the symbolic resonances of the colour green. Rossetti

and his friends were experimenting with both possibilities: the non-symbolising symbol and the proliferating symbol. Both were rebellions against well-established conventions for pictorial symbolism. Indeed, both made a radical challenge to the very notion that there are stable meanings attached to the objects and events of the real world. This could seem to threaten the most basic assumptions on which the Victorian social and political order rested.

The Beloved is instantly recognisable as a Rossetti, but it also bears the traces of artistic cameraderie within the circle, incorporating the features of Sandys's gipsy friend Keomi, in the figure on the right, and the accessories borrowed from Boyce. Another distinctive aspect of the collecting habit in the Rossetti circle was the way objects were borrowed and swapped. This recalls the relaxed attitude toward personal property in the French myth of the Bohemian life; Bohemian artists might pawn their possessions to help their friends, borrow each other's dress coats for important occasions, or appropriate each other's furniture for firewood. Countless letters among the artists in the Rossetti circle record their requests to borrow objects for use in pictures.

But the artists did not just share possessions; they shared compositional formulae for their pictures and even physical types for the figures. The bow-shaped lips, long necks, and rippling hair that we now associate most readily with Rossetti also appeared in the work of Burne-Jones, Sandys, Solomon, and others. At times this could cause tension; Rossetti believed that Sandys had imitated his *Helen of Troy* too closely (figs. 18, 19), and a rift developed between the two artists. This was the closest Sandys ever came to Rossetti, and was perhaps misjudged; but Sandys was only carrying a step too far what was basic to the circle's distinctive identity. The rippling hair and full lips functioned as talismans in much the same way as the hair ornaments and pieces of china. They were symbols, in a general sense, of the group's shared artistic project; more specifically they were symbols of the group's compelling shared image of woman. The Rossettian image of woman has been criticised for its repetitiveness; but repetition was precisely its hallmark.

fig.19 J.A.M. Whistler **Three Figures: Pink and Grey** 1868–78
oil on canvas 139.7 × 185.4 cm
Tate Gallery

fig.20 D.G. Rossetti **Fazio's Mistress (Aurelia)** 1863
(detail of fig.20)

Symbolising Woman

A recurring image in the work of the Rossetti circle was that of a woman absorbed in self-contemplation, gazing into a mirror or combing her hair. Such activities emphasised the talismanic parts of the female body that were repeated in picture after picture: eyes, lips, hands, rippling hair. At one level these must be called symbols of eroticism. Their symbolic reference is not so much to the characteristics of the depicted woman as to those of male desire, as the feminist art historian Griselda Pollock has explored with particular forcefulness in her book *Vision and Difference*.

An early example is Rossetti's *Fazio's Mistress* of 1863 (fig.20), painted in the rich Venetian-inspired oil colours that had first appeared in *Bocca Baciata* four years earlier. Here the very title encourages the spectator to view the woman through the eyes of a man, the fourteenth-century Italian poet Fazio degli Uberti, whose poem about his mistress had been translated by Rossetti for his first published volume, *The Early Italian Poets* of 1861. More precisely, the poem is about Fazio *looking* at his mistress; it begins, in Rossetti's translation:

> I look at the crisp golden-threaded hair
> Whereof, to thrall my heart, Love twists a net...

The power relations here are complex: the male poet declares himself enslaved by the woman's beauty, yet the woman can exert this power only as a result of the male's act of looking at her. A similar complexity is characteristic of this and other paintings of women, presented as powerful in erotic appeal, but only by virtue of the male painter's representational activity, analogous to Fazio's poetic gaze. The poet's lines may have suggested Rossetti's motif of the woman plaiting her hair, and Rossetti also illustrates the other features of the woman, as observed by Fazio: 'I look into her eyes... I look at the amorous beautiful mouth... I look at her white easy neck'. One source, then, for the pictures' talismanic body parts was the early Italian love poetry of Rossetti's translations. The repetitive poetic imagery of 'Dante and his Circle', as Rossetti entitled a section of his collection of 1861, is paralleled by the equally repetitive pictorial imagery of Rossetti and his circle.

When he republished the translations in 1873, Rossetti used the title *Dante and his Circle* for the whole volume, tendentiously positing a poetic movement under the leadership of his namesake Dante, but also reflecting his own circle's interest in masculine cameraderie as a focus for artistic creativity. By that date, the theme of a woman contemplating her own beauty was a well-established element in the circle's repertoire. Simeon Solomon transferred the theme to a classical setting in his picture of 1869, *The Toilette of a Roman Lady* (fig.21). Nor had the theme lost its resonance in the 1890s, when Aubrey Beardsley chose it for one of his illustrations to Oscar Wilde's play, *Salome* (fig.22).

fig.20 D.G. Rossetti **Fazio's Mistress (Aurelia)** 1863
oil on canvas 43.2 × 36.8 cm

In Whistler's variation on the theme, *The Little White Girl* of 1864 (fig.23), the woman does not quite meet her own gaze in the mirror. Nonetheless, the lines written by Swinburne in response to the picture, and pasted by Whistler to its frame, stress her self-contemplation:

> I watch my face, and wonder
> At my bright hair…

Swinburne's poem echoes that of Fazio, but here it is the woman who looks, not the male poet. That might suggest a feminist reading, where the woman takes control of a traditional male preserve, the act of looking. However, the woman's act of looking, in Swinburne's poem, is strangely inconclusive. Contemplating her reflection, she asks:

> Art thou the ghost, my sister,
> White sister there,
> Am I the ghost, who knows?

The gazing female's inability to attain self-knowledge might be a metaphor for woman's political powerlessness in Victorian society; or it might be a projection of the male artist's emphasis, whether paranoid or pleasurable, on woman's unfathomability. In either case the lines make an apt comment on a painting that was, by Victorian standards, full of mysteries: vague in narrative content, sketchy in execution, and puzzlingly eclectic in its accessories, including a Japanese fan, a blue-and-white vase, an unstructured white dress of no particular fashion, and a conventional London fireplace.

Swinburne's emphasis on the figure's pleasure in her own beauty hints at another implication for the pictures of female self-contemplation: eroticism and narcissism combine to hint at a topic of contemporary concern, female masturbation. With his taste for unconventional sexuality of any kind, Swinburne may well have been aware of the contemporary medical literature on the dangers of female autoeroticism. Much of this literature now reads as the most

fig.21 Simeon Solomon
The Toilette of a Roman Lady 1869
oil on canvas 113 × 97.2 cm, Private Collection

fig.22 Aubrey Beardsley **The Toilette of Salome** 1893
pen, ink, and wash on paper 22.7 × 16.2 cm
Trustees of the British Museum

fig.23 J.A.M. Whistler **The Little White Girl: Symphony in White No.2** 1864
oil on canvas 76.5 × 51.1 cm
Tate Gallery

fig.24 D.G. Rossetti **Lady Lilith** 1864–8 (repainted 1872–3)
oil on canvas 95.3 × 81.3 cm
Delaware Art Museum, Wilmington. Samuel and Mary R. Bancroft Memorial

blatant Victorian misogyny, but attitudes may have been more complex in the 'Bohemian' artistic circles that prided themselves on freedom from contemporary moral conventions. As the cultural historian Bram Dijkstra has shown, Victorian doctors claimed that female masturbation led to enervation and ill health. The languid poses and pale, drawn features of many of the depicted women may relate at some level to this medical stereotype. If the pictures betray male fear of woman's sexual self-sufficiency, they do so with equal admixture of fascination with the idea.

Languor is a principal characteristic of Rossetti's *Lady Lilith* (fig.24), where the figure gazes into a mirror she seems almost too tired to hold, while her dress slips to reveal the talismanic Rossetti neck, a pale shoulder, and the swelling of an ample bosom. Again the cue seems to have been a literary source linking a woman's sexual power with her hair. Rossetti picked up an obscure reference to Lilith, the legendary wife of Adam before the creation of Eve, in Goethe's *Faust*. Swinburne's description of the picture, in his article of 1868 on contemporary painting, cites Shelley's translation of Goethe's lines:

> She excels
> All women in the magic of her locks;
> And when she winds them round a young man's
>   neck
> She will not ever set him free again.

Lady Lilith is, at least superficially, the most obvious example of what has come to be called the *femme fatale*, fascinating through sexual danger. As the American scholar Virginia M. Allen has documented, the Lilith of legend was an epitome of female evil, a murderess of babies. Moreover, she was the first female rebel against male authority, refusing to obey Adam. The contemporary relevance of this aspect of the Lilith legend was elaborated in a letter to Rossetti from an otherwise unknown correspondent, one Ponsonby A. Lyons, later published by W.M. Rossetti in the volume *Rossetti Papers 1862 to 1870*. Lyons advises: 'Lilith … was

evidently the first strong-minded woman and the original advocate of women's rights. At present she is a queen of the demons'. In stray comments on the picture, Rossetti and his friends repeatedly described it as representing, not the Lilith of immemorial antiquity, but a distinctively modern Lilith, dressed in a modern gown. That might suggest a link between the subject and the contemporary women's rights movement. Rossetti's comment in a letter of 1870 draws together the themes of Lilith's modernity, her autoeroticism, and her sexual power: the picture, he writes, 'represents a *Modern Lilith* combing out her abundant golden hair and gazing on herself in the glass with that complete self-absorption by whose fascination such natures draw others within their circle'. The misogynistic overtones are apparently confirmed by the next sentence, describing the central idea as 'the perilous principle in the world being female from the first'. However, Lilith's rebellion against male authority could also be interpreted as an analogue for the Bohemian project of rebellion against conventional social rules. And Rossetti's celebration of female wickedness could be read as a protest against Victorian stereotypes of feminine virtue.

For Swinburne, Lilith's fascination was not precisely wickedness, but utter freedom from morality either good or evil. In his account Lilith becomes a metaphor for art's independence from conventional morality, a conspicuous aspect of the Bohemian creed: 'Of evil desire or evil impulse she has nothing; and nothing of good'. Lilith also stands, in Swinburne's review, for the physical extreme of the archetypal divide between physical and spiritual: 'For this serene and sublime sorceress there is no life but of the body; with spirit (if spirit there be) she can dispense'. This divide applies equally, in Swinburne's context, to the nature of woman and the nature of art.

That dual reference, to woman and art, also characterises the sonnet Rossetti wrote to accompany the picture, later titled 'Body's Beauty' and paired with another sonnet called 'Soul's Beauty', in its turn associated with a painting, *Sibylla Palmifera* (fig.25). The two pairs of sonnets and pictures can easily be interpreted as symbolising the conventional Victorian dichotomy between Madonna and Magdalen, wife and whore. They can also be read as symbolising the dichotomy between the spiritual and physical in art. However, in Swinburne's aesthetics there was no moral choice to be made between the two, and perhaps Rossetti's pictures also refuse to offer a clear choice; the symbols of virtue and vice are oddly assorted between the two images. The sonnet for *Lady Lilith* identifies her attributes as the rose and the poppy, traditional symbols, respectively, of love and death, seemingly indicating the mortal danger attached to sensual love. But the rose and poppy appear prominently also in *Sibylla Palmifera*, on either side of the figure's head. Perhaps it is because she is a deceiver that Lilith wears the trappings of virtue: a virginal white dress, with the white daisies of innocence in her lap, and white roses behind. Paradoxically, the red rose and red robe of passion belong instead to *Sibylla Palmifera*. In Swinburne's description, it is she who wields power over love and death, with the palm in her hand as sceptre.

The complexity of Rossetti's symbolism defies reduction to a simple message. The two pictures, with their sonnets, propose a dichotomy, yet the terms of that dichotomy prove elusive. The two images end by dismantling their own apparent premise; at the basic level of visual appearance, they at least as similar as they are dichotomous. As Swinburne put it, *Sibylla Palmifera* is 'as ripe and firm of flesh as her softer and splendid sister'.

Rossetti has often been accused of repetitiveness in his compositional formulae, still more in his female physical types; the artists of his circle are open still more to the charge of repeating types now seen as Rossetti's personal property. But the repetition of the formula, in both *Lady Lilith* and *Sibylla Palmifera*, might threaten the conventional boundary between female virtue and female vice: which is the saint, which is the witch? And which should we prefer? If the pictures leave the viewer in doubt, that may be their challenge to the dichotomy between wife and whore.

fig.25 D.G. Rossetti **Sibylla Palmifera** 1866–70
oil on canvas 98.4 × 85 cm
Board of Trustees of the National Museums and Galleries
on Merseyside (Lady Lever Art Gallery, Port Sunlight)

THE ROSSETTI CIRCLE IN PUBLIC

Swinburne's article on contemporary painting was published as if it were a perfectly ordinary review of the Royal Academy exhibition of 1868. But Swinburne used the article as an opportunity to describe works by members of the Rossetti circle that for one reason or another did not appear before the public that thronged to the Academy. His extended discussion of Rossetti's non-exhibited pictures was quoted above; he also devoted considerable space to Whistler's unfinished and unexhibited works of this period, and to Frederick Sandys's *Medea* (fig.26), which the Hanging Committee of the Royal Academy in 1868 had declined to hang, although it had been passed by the Selection Committee.

Sandys's picture features an ancient Greek analogue for Lilith: Medea, the mythological sorceress who murdered her own children. Moreover, the figure is provided with a range of talismanic accessories, among them Egyptian animal motifs, Japanese-inspired flying cranes, a dragon that appears Far Eastern, and a coral necklace similar to examples found in Rossetti's pictures. We do not know whether the Academy's reluctance to hang the picture represented resistance to the Rossetti circle's celebration of women whom convention would class as evil, or to the use of puzzling or anachronistic accessories; *Medea* was accepted and hung on resubmission to the next Academy exhibition, that of 1869. Since Rossetti never submitted his paintings to the juries of public exhibitions, we shall never know whether they would have been acceptable. What is clear is that exhibited works by other members of the circle were treated, by contemporary art critics, as rebellions against conventional practices in painting.

The press response to Burne-Jones's watercolours, exhibited at the Old Water-Colour Society, is a case in point. On Burne-Jones's first public appearance in 1864, the critic for the *Saturday Review* called his work 'an exaggerated protest against contemporary superficiality and prettyism' – stronger stuff, in other words, than the ordinary run of English watercolours. That response was partly due to Burne-Jones's unusual watercolour technique. The English watercolour tradition was a considerable source of national pride; even continental art critics, ordinarily condescending toward English painting, conceded English pre-eminence

fig.26 Frederick Sandys **Medea** 1866–8
oil on panel 62.2 × 46.3 cm
Birmingham Museums and Art Gallery

fig.27 Edward Burne-Jones **Green Summer** 1864
opaque watercolour 29 × 48.3 cm
Private Collection

in the watercolour medium. But Burne-Jones rejected the transparent colours and fluid handling seen as characteristic of the English watercolour tradition. Instead he used opaque, vibrant colours, densely worked in a fashion that many critics thought more suitable to oil paint than watercolour. The technique was derived from that of Rossetti, developed in the 1850s. Since Rossetti's watercolours had rarely been exhibited outside his own studio, Burne-Jones's technique came as a novelty in the mid-1860s.

Burne-Jones's exhibits at the Old Water-Colour Society in 1865 made a dramatic impact. Critics called them 'abortions', 'impertinences', 'monstrosities', 'perversities',

'preternatural eccentricities'. These seem strange words to apply to a picture such as *Green Summer* (fig.27), with its idyllic subject matter, harmonious green colouring, and rhythmic curvilinear patterning. But the critic for the *Art Journal*, the leading art periodical of the period, saw the picture as an outrage against established practices in watercolour painting. To this critic, accustomed to the sharply differentiated local colour of most contemporary painting, it was inadmissable to limit the range of colours to variations of green: 'why is it that he has woven the robes of the picnic party out of the green grass whereon they sit, thus bidding defiance to known laws of chromatic art'? Moreover, the

fig.28 Walter Crane **The White Knight** 1870
watercolour on paper 45.7 × 61 cm
Private Collection

fig.29 Robert Bateman **The Dead Knight** *c.*1870
watercolour on paper 28 × 39 cm
Robin de Beaumont

drapery folds seemed to be organised into artful curves regardless of the forms of the body underneath, and defiant even of 'the well-ascertained laws of gravity'. Both the colour scheme and the linear patterns, then, appeared so obviously contrived by the artist as to be not merely unconventional, but actually against nature; hence the language of abortion and deformity.

Perhaps the critic was also disturbed by the undifferentiated characterisations of the figures, analogous to the uniformity of colour and repetition of line. The figures do not have individual roles to play in a narrative or drama, as critics expected of multiple-figure compositions. The loss of specific symbolic coding, observed above in the painters' use of accessories, here extends to the figures; critics could not decode the roles of the individual figures to arrive at a specific narrative or even a well-defined dramatic situation. Instead of displaying different narrative roles, emotions, or characters, all of the figures share the same languorous mood. At some level this may have suggested the enervation associated with sexual self-indulgence. The composition, with the women arranged in a self-contained circle, may even hint at the communal autoeroticism associated by some Victorian doctors with girls' boarding schools. This appears to be a secret society of women, absorbed in dreams that are never revealed to the spectator.

For many critics, the absence of specific narrative or symbolic meaning seemed dangerously anarchic. But for the twenty-year-old artist Walter Crane, the narrative vagueness opened up a new realm for the imagination, exciting precisely because it was not bound by established patterns for reading meaning from pictures. In his later reminiscences, Crane described the effect of Burne-Jones's work on himself and his artist friends:

> The curtain had been lifted, and we had had a glimpse into a magic world of romance and pictured poetry, peopled with ghosts of 'ladies dead and lovely knights,' – a twilight world of dark mysterious woodlands, haunted streams, meads of deep green starred with burning flowers, veiled in a dim and mystic light, and stained with low-toned crimson and gold, as if indeed one had gazed through the glass of
> > Magic casements opening on the foam
> > Of perilous seas in faerylands forlorn.

For Crane, Burne-Jones's work suggested the possibility of proliferating symbolism, leading the imagination in fascinating new directions rather than confining it to a one-to-one interpretation.

As a result of his exhibits at the Old Water-Colour Society, Burne-Jones began to attract followers of his own, among them Crane and his friend Robert Bateman. Crane's *The White Knight* (fig.28) and Bateman's *The Dead Knight* (fig.29) emphasise the symbolic resonances the young artists found so powerful in Burne-Jones's medievalism. In both pictures the solitary knight is dwarfed by a 'mysterious woodland' that helps to create mood in the absence of specific narrative. Perhaps Crane's knight is on a quest; if so, its goal is unrevealed, nor is there any hint of the cause of the death of Bateman's knight. Viewers are free to imagine any number of narratives to account for the depicted situations.

By the later 1860s critics were writing of a distinctive school, led by Burne-Jones. The circle was thus expanding to include artists who had no close social connections with Rossetti, but who were seen by critics to be defying the conventional rules for clear narratives, intelligible symbolism, and even solid craftsmanship. The artists were frequently taken to task for technical shortcomings. The critic Emily Pattison, writing in the *Westminster Review* in 1869, dubbed the artists of Crane's subcircle the 'poetry-without-grammar school', complaining with some justice that the young artists neglected accurate drawing in favour of expressiveness. But her description of their works as 'mere fancies, hints, sketches, possibilities of pictures' hints at the notion of the proliferating symbol. It was just such suggestiveness that the artists prized as leading the imagination farther and deeper than cut-and-dried narrative

fig.30 Simeon Solomon **Heliogabalus, High Priest of the Sun** 1866
watercolour on paper 46.4 × 29.2 cm
The Forbes Magazine Collection, New York

painting. The 'correct' drawing of the Royal Academy Schools might be one of the conventions scorned by the true Bohemian. Neither Rossetti nor Burne-Jones had much formal training, but both artists found ways to turn their technical deficiencies to expressive advantage.

An important forum was the Dudley Gallery, formed in 1865 and particularly welcoming to young and inexperienced artists. Both Crane and Bateman were frequent exhibitors at the Dudley, but even more prominent was an artist closely associated with Rossetti, Swinburne, and Burne-Jones: Simeon Solomon. Solomon's personal conduct was perhaps the most deliberately unconventional of all the members of the Rossetti circle. Even before his arrest and conviction in 1873 for homosexual activities, he seems to have had little interest in conforming to contemporary conventions for respectable middle-class behaviour. After 1873 he was ostracised even by his fellow-connoisseur of pornography, Swinburne, but he adopted the role of social outcast with some pride, refusing the aid of his wealthy Jewish relatives. This was an extreme of the Bohemian image, partly enforced by circumstances, but also demonstrating a personal integrity nourished by the myth of Bohemianism.

At the Dudley Gallery in 1868, Solomon showed the watercolour *Heliogabalus, High Priest of the Sun* (fig.30), a subject as arcane as Rossetti's *Lady Lilith*, and with similar moral ambiguities. Heliogabalus was a historical figure, a Roman Emperor of the third century A.D. renowned for his extreme decadence. Like Lilith, Heliogabalus was a symbol of hyperbolic evil, but also of overwhelming personal beauty, emphasised in the ancient accounts of his reign. Here the Emperor appears in his role as high priest of the Syrian sun god, whose worship he introduced at Rome. This permits a dazzling array of talismanic accessories, mingling the symbolism of diverse religions. Swinburne's account of the picture, in an article on Solomon published in 1871, emphasises the dichotomies in Solomon's presentation of the figure who is both Emperor and priest, 'symbolic in that strange union of offices at once of east and west, of ghostly glory and visible lordship, of the lusts of the flesh and the secrets of the soul, of the kingdom of this world and the mystery of another'. On this interpretation, the picture combines the resonances of *Lady Lilith* and *Sibylla Palmifera* into a single figure.

Perhaps tactfully, Swinburne omits to mention the principal dichotomy, that between male and female; the more erudite among the picture's viewers would have known of Heliogabalus's transvestitism, his self-appointed title 'Empress of Rome', and his lovers of both sexes. Solomon redeploys the Rossettian talismans of female eroticism to create a figure of androgynous beauty: the introspective gaze, the sensual mouth, the languid pose.

Contemporary critics admired Solomon's skill at painting exotic accessories, but his androgynous male figures were controversial. In 1870, the critic for the *Spectator* briefly indulged the hope that Solomon was presenting his 'degenerate creatures in men's attire' to elicit the spectator's disgust, and thus 'pointing a wholesome moral'; on further consideration, though, the critic decided that was unlikely. Solomon's androgynous male figures challenged contemporary notions of masculinity; critical responses show just how serious that challenge was felt to be. His female figures could make a reciprocal challenge, as in *The Toilette of a Roman Lady* (fig.21), where a female figure who appeared unequivocally masculine to critics was engaged in the quintessentially feminine activity of making her toilet.

Solomon's paintings were in some respects the most daring productions of the Rossetti circle. Yet his work appeared not only at the Dudley Gallery, but at the Royal Academy, the most traditional art institution in Britain. Despite Rossetti's self-imposed isolation from the public sphere, the work of his circle was a conspicuous element in the art world, although not always a comfortable one.

fig.31 Simeon Solomon **Bacchus** 1867
oil on paper laid onto canvas 50.8 × 37.5 cm
Birmingham Museums and Art Gallery

ART FOR ART'S SAKE

Swinburne, Blake, and Aesthetic Philosophy

Simeon Solomon was aware of a tradition in aesthetic theory that identified the androgyne with the ideal in art, a notion that was also important in continental Symbolist circles later in the century. In a letter of the late 1860s, Solomon defended his androgynous figures as rising above the merely animal nature of either man or woman, to attain a purified, sexless spirituality. This philosophical defence is reminiscent of Swinburne's account of *Lady Lilith* and *Sibylla Palmifera*, as emblematic of the art-theoretical duality of body and soul.

fig.32 D.G. Rossetti **Algernon Charles Swinburne** 1860
pencil on paper 23.5 × 19.7 cm
Private Collection

Both Solomon and Swinburne might be accused of hypocrisy – claiming purely aesthetic justification for powerfully erotic images. But in another sense it was precisely the relationship between aesthetic purity and sensuality that was being explored.

Swinburne was the key figure in promoting the philosophical ideas of the Rossetti circle (fig.32). It was he who introduced the term 'art for art's sake' in what seems at first an odd context, his study of *William Blake*, ready for publication by the end of 1867 but not finally circulated until August 1868. Blake had, however, been a figure of particular interest in the Rossetti circle for some years, since both Rossetti brothers had collaborated on the publication of the biography of Blake, left unfinished on the death of its original author Alexander Gilchrist. The obscurity of meaning in some of Blake's poems led Rossetti to muse on the potential independence of some purely poetic quality from rational meaning. As he wrote to Gilchrist's widow in February 1863:

> The truth is that as regards such a poem as [Blake's] *My Spectre* I do not understand it a bit better than anybody else, only I know better than some may know that it has claims as poetry, apart from the question of understanding it, and is therefore worth printing.

Rossetti's work on Blake, then, was one factor in his exploration of the complex possible relations between a symbol and the concept it might (or might not) symbolise.

It is interesting that Swinburne chose Blake for his most thorough elaboration of art for art's sake, a notion that has usually been considered French in origin. Indeed, Swinburne wove his idiosyncratic interpretation of Blake together with numerous references to the French champions of art for art's sake, Charles Baudelaire and Théophile Gautier. Nonetheless, when he published his meditations on the nature of art he chose to do so in the context of William Blake, the English painter-poet closely identified with Rossetti.

But what did Swinburne mean by 'art for art's sake'? The study of Blake dates from the most radical phase of Swinburne's youth. It is a vehement polemic against contemporary notions of art's responsibilities, either to moral orthodoxy or to factual accuracy: 'Handmaid of religion, exponent of duty, servant of fact, pioneer of morality, [Art] cannot in any way become; she would be none of these things though you were to bray her in a mortar'. This is an extreme statement of the Bohemian creed: art's purity or integrity depends on the rejection of all conventional rules.

More specifically, Swinburne rejects all links between art and the moral or intellectual realms. Art's own realm he identifies as 'beauty', a realm of the senses as opposed to either the intellect or the moral faculty. But there was considerable latitude in the interpretation of this notion of an art of the senses, as will become obvious below. Did art for art's sake mean a hermetic art of purely formal perfection, divested of any reference to ideas beyond the picture frame? In that case, aesthetic purity would demand non-symbolising symbolism, where the forms on the canvas stood for nothing beyond their pure visual appearance. Or did art for art's sake mean an art of sensuous plenitude, more powerful in its impact because unmediated by the intellect or moral faculty? In that case, aesthetic purity could encompass proliferating symbolism, where the visible forms could suggest multiple meanings beyond mundane rationality.

Perhaps deliberately, Swinburne's discussions of 'beauty', in *William Blake* and his other writings, leave those questions unanswered. Indeed, the theoretical writings of Swinburne and others associated with the Rossetti circle served less to establish guidelines for art than to open up the possibility of an art that was non-rational and non-moral. It remained for the artists to explore what an art of the senses might entail.

The Holland Park Circle

Despite its growing press image as an esoteric sect, the Rossetti circle was not alone in its explorations of aesthetic theory. Rossetti and his friends had particularly close contacts to an artistic circle in another London suburb, the area now called Holland Park. Since 1850, George Frederic Watts had lived at Little Holland House, on the estate of Lord and Lady Holland, as the perpetual guest of a wealthy family called Prinsep. The Prinseps' social aspirations centred on the formation of a literary and artistic salon; their regular guests included Tennyson, Thackeray, Robert and Elizabeth Browning, and others. Later in the 1850s, Frederic Leighton added glamour to the Prinseps' salon; independently wealthy and well connected, he rose rapidly to eminence as a painter. On his election in 1864 to the Associateship of the Royal Academy, he began to build a sumptuous studio house on a site near Little Holland House. Leighton's artistic training in Germany, Rome, and Paris had given cosmopolitan polish to his manners, his art, and his ideas on aesthetics. The discussions on art and art theory in the Holland Park circle are more scantily documented than those of the Rossetti circle. But Leighton, better educated and more widely travelled than any other English artist of his generation, must have contributed much to the debates on art not only at Little Holland House, but in the Rossetti circle as well.

The later reputations of Watts and Leighton, as pillars of the Victorian art establishment, make them seem a world away from the 'Bohemian' circle of Rossetti and his friends; the most familiar images of the Holland Park artists show them in their grand studios, surrounded by the trappings of wealth and social eminence (figs. 33, 34). No doubt there was a discernible difference, from the start, between the patrician tone in Holland Park and Rossetti's unconventional ménage at Tudor House. Nonetheless, contacts between the two groups were frequent and friendly; the diaries of George Price Boyce and William Michael Rossetti record many meetings. Not only were Rossetti's friends

fig.33 J.P. Mayall
George Frederic Watts in his Studio *c*.1884
photogravure, courtesy of the British Library

fig.34 J.P. Mayall
Frederic Leighton in his Studio *c*.1884
photogravure, courtesy of the British Library

frequently in evidence at Little Holland House, but the fastidious Leighton and Watts even visited Rossetti, on occasion, in the insalubrious surroundings of Tudor House. Moreover, the Holland Park circle was just as opposed to conventional respectability as Rossetti's circle, although in a different way. The illustrator George Du Maurier, later an acute satirist of fashionable aestheticism in his drawings for *Punch* (fig.53), noted 'an atmosphere of looseness about this aristocratic lot' when he visited Little Holland House in the early 1860s; there were rumours about love affairs between Leighton and women in high society. As different as the two circles were, they were united in their scorn for Victorian bourgeois conventions, including the conventions of Victorian art.

Art critics who had contacts in both circles spoke of their work in close conjunction. The article of 1868, in which Swinburne enthused over the unexhibited work of Rossetti, Whistler, and Sandys, began with a eulogy of Watts and another artist associated with the Holland Park group, Albert Moore. Indeed, Swinburne's description of Moore's *Azaleas* (fig.35), shown at the Royal Academy in 1868, makes the picture into the quintessential example of art for art's sake, linking it with the French version of the theory:

> His painting is to artists what the verse of Théophile Gautier is to poets; the faultless and secure expression of an exclusive worship of things formally beautiful. That contents them; they leave to others the labours and the joys of thought or passion.

The statuesque grandeur of the figure and the restricted palette of Moore's picture distinguish it from the pulsating sensuality and intense hues of Rossetti's pictures of women. But Moore, too, introduces anachronistic pottery into his classicising scene, and the figure's expressionless gaze might be called an icier version of Rossettian female introspection. To conclude his account of the picture, Swinburne draws on a significant element of the aesthetic ideas that were exchanged

fig.35 Albert Moore **Azaleas** exh.1868
oil on canvas 198.1 × 100.3 cm
The Hugh Lane Municipal Gallery of Modern Art, Dublin

between the two artistic circles, a notional analogy between painting and music:

> The melody of colour, the symphony of form is complete: one more beautiful thing is achieved, one more delight is born into the world; and its meaning is beauty; and its reason for being is to be.

The Condition of Music

> All art constantly aspires towards the condition of music.
> *Walter Pater*

Walter Pater's famous dictum was not published until 1877, when it appeared in his article on Venetian Renaissance painting, 'The School of Giorgione'. That article tied together two strands that had long been present in the art of both the Rossetti and the Holland Park circles: an interest in the Venetian Renaissance, discussed above in the context of Rossetti's *Bocca Baciata* of 1859 (fig.8), and an interest in music that dated back at least as far. Rossetti himself made the link between Venetian painting and music in his picture of 1872, *Veronica Veronese* (fig.1); the figure, in sumptuous Venetian costume, listens to the song of a bird whose notes she listlessly reproduces on the viol hanging before her. In fact the link between Venetian painting and music was much older, a stock element in traditional art theory, based on the notion of sensuous address. Colour, the key characteristic ascribed to the Venetians, was often said to address the eye in the same fashion as music addresses the ear.

An early exploration of that notion of sensory address is Leighton's *Lieder Ohne Worte* (fig.36), or 'Songs Without Words', shown at the Royal Academy in 1861. The figure is one of the most languorous of the period; her sallow skin and dark-circled eyes appeared diseased to some critics, who also noted the gesture with which she caresses her own bare foot. Whether it was his intention or not, Leighton came close to creating an iconography of female autoeroticism in this work. Certainly intentional, though, was the sensuous emphasis of the subject matter: the figure abandons herself to pure sensory experience, listening to the sound of birdsong and flowing water, the 'songs without words' of the title. Moreover, Leighton proposed an analogy between the (auditory) sensuous experience of the figure *in* the picture, and the (visual) sensuous experience of the spectator *of* the

Frederic Leighton **Lieder Ohne Worte** *c.*1860–1 (detail of fig.36)

fig.36 Frederic Leighton **Lieder Ohne Worte** *c.*1860–1
oil on canvas 101.7 × 63 cm
Tate Gallery

fig.37 Edward Burne-Jones **The Madness of Sir Tristram** 1862
opaque watercolour on paper 59 × 55 cm
Private Collection

picture. As he put it in a letter of 1861, 'I have endeavoured, both by colour and by flowing delicate forms, to translate to the eye of the spectator something of the pleasure which the child receives through her ears'.

Leighton's German title repeats that of a series of piano pieces by Mendelssohn, literally songs without words since they have no vocal line. The German-educated Leighton may well have known of Mendelssohn's ideas about how the pure sound of music conveys meanings that are independent of the intellectualism of spoken language. His title declares a similar aim for his own picture, a scene set in no particular time or place, and without definite narrative or symbolism, but conveying its meaning through colour and 'flowing delicate forms'. Leighton had spent much of the later 1850s in Paris, and may also have been familiar with French notions of 'synaesthesia', or the evocation of one kind of sensory experience through the medium of another. The most famous expression of such theories is Baudelaire's poem 'Correspondences', which invokes the sensory experiences of perfumes, sounds, and colours through the medium of poetic language.

The French theories were also familiar in the Rossetti circle, through Swinburne's fascination with the writings of Baudelaire and Gautier. Characteristically, Rossetti and his friends often evoked the sensory experience of music through the visual representation of exotic musical instruments, one of their collecting interests. Burne-Jones's watercolour of 1862, *The Madness of Sir Tristram* (fig.37), places music-making in a narrative context, representing the knight of Arthurian legend, driven mad by a report of his lady's infidelity and playing an archaic harp. Here the sound of music is invoked to heighten the emotional tension, assisted also by the intense colour of Burne-Jones's early watercolour style.

Calmer and more measured is the musicality of *The Lament* of 1866 (fig.38), in which the narrative has become enigmatic: the male figure bends in apparent grief as the female holds a strangely shaped medieval instrument, but their relationship is unclear. The roses shedding their petals perhaps symbolise the loss of love. The empty courtyard behind the figures appears partly overgrown with delicate foliage, suggesting but not quite specifying a theme of loss or decay. The subject of *The Lament*, then, may be not dissimilar to that of *The Madness of Sir Tristram*, again using music to express despair in love. But the later watercolour no longer relies on an extraneous legend, or even precise symbols within the picture. Instead, the measured spaces of the architecture suggest the measured intervals of the music in a synaesthetic fashion analogous to Leighton's claim for *Lieder Ohne Worte*. The picture conveys its meaning in what Swinburne might have considered purely artistic terms, through the immediately visible elements of design and colour. As with *Lieder Ohne Worte*, the spectator need not decode the image intellectually, to arrive at a narrative or message; indeed, such an effort would result in disappointment. Instead, the spectator must either rest content with the measured intervals of space and colour, as non-symbolising symbols, or invent meanings for the depicted elements, as proliferating symbols.

fig.38 Edward Burne-Jones **The Lament** 1864–6
opaque watercolour on paper 47.5 × 79.5 cm
William Morris Gallery (London Borough of Waltham Forest)

47

Pygmalion

Pictures with music-making subject matter fulfilled the demand for aesthetic purity in a special way: they *were* art, but they were also *about* art. Notionally, then, there was no gap between the sensory experience of the painting and the significance of its subject matter. The subject of a woman gazing into a mirror, explored above, might be given a similar interpretation: the subject is *about* visual beauty, as the picture is itself an example of the visually beautiful.

Artists might also choose traditional subjects, from Christian or classical legend, that centred on beauty or artistic creation. An obvious candidate was the myth of Pygmalion, the ancient sculptor who created a statue of a woman so beautiful that he fell in love with it; eventually the goddess of love, Venus, took pity on the sculptor and brought the statue to life as a real woman, Galatea. Watts's interpretation of the myth (fig.39), exhibited at the Royal Academy in 1868, omitted Pygmalion to show only the statue in a head-and-shoulders format with a floral background, reminiscent of Rossetti's pictures; the statue is just beginning to come to life, as colour infuses the talismanic body parts, lips, eyes, rippling hair, exposed nipple. The symbolic equation of the beauty of the woman with that of her floral accessories is particularly evident in Watts's picture, where the suggestive brushwork of the flowers makes them start forward, seeming to brush the figure's cheek and echoing the tint of her hair. Like Rossetti's *Fazio's Mistress*, the picture plays on the question of who creates: do we see the 'real' Galatea or the creation of Pygmalion – or the creation of Watts?

At about the same date, William Morris was composing a poem based on the Pygmalion myth, for which Burne-Jones was to design illustrations; the complete set of illustrations was never realised, but four of them became an independent series of oil paintings. The narrative exposition of the subject, in four successive episodes, might seem to contradict the move away from narrative specificity of this period, but it also indicates the exceptional importance of the subject in Burne-Jones's oeuvre; indeed, he executed another complete

fig.39 G.F. Watts **The Wife of Pygmalion** 1868
oil on canvas 67.3 × 53.3 cm
Faringdon Collection Trust, Buscot Park, Oxfordshire

figs.40–43
Edward Burne-Jones **Pygmalion and the Image I–IV** *c*.1868–78
Birmingham Museums and Art Gallery

48

fig.40 **Pygmalion and the Image I:**
The Heart Desires
oil on canvas 99 × 76.3 cm

fig.41 **Pygmalion and the Image II:**
The Hand Refrains
oil on canvas 98.7 × 76.3 cm

fig.42 **Pygmalion and the Image III:**
The Godhead Fires
oil on canvas 99.1 × 76.5 cm

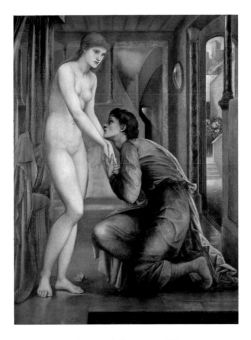

fig.43 **Pygmalion and the Image IV:**
The Soul Attains
oil on canvas 99.4 × 76.6 cm

series of four Pygmalion pictures, with differences of detail, in the later 1870s (figs.40–43).

If the four sequential images promise narrative development, they also withhold it. The compositions repeat each other, with the figures trading places from scene to scene, as if continually testing the spectator to ask whether anything has changed, or whether all has stayed the same. The teasing changes of detail in the settings, from picture to picture, function similarly; round arches are exchanged for square ones, a rectilinear staircase for a curving one, so that the spectator cannot be sure whether or not the four scenes occur in the same time and place. The four pictures, certainly designed as a series, suggest that the Rossetti circle's repetitive imagery was not merely a commercial expedient, repeating popular compositions for as many buyers as possible. It could be turned to aesthetic advantage, urging the spectator to wonder whether the same visible forms need symbolise the same underlying meanings, or whether symbols can change their significance without warning.

In yet another play on repetition, Pygmalion and the statue resemble each other facially, becoming androgynous in the fashion of Burne-Jones's close associate in the later 1860s, Simeon Solomon. This might be interpreted as a sign of Victorian misogyny: the ideal female figure has no existence except as a reflection, indeed a repetition, of her male creator. The statue might be described as a symbol of male yearning for a female fashioned to his own specifications. But the mirroring imagery can work in the opposite direction. The male artist, as he shrinks in awe of the statue's beauty, appears a mere reflection of the purity of the artistic ideal he can create only partially. It requires the intervention of the goddess Venus, in the third image, to realise the artist's ideal. This draws on a traditional element in art theory, to which Burne-Jones repeatedly referred in private conversations: the perennial failure of the created work to live up to the purity of the aesthetic ideal. The haunting quality of the series as a whole, with its repetitive alternations between the figures of creator and created, is as much a meditation on the male creator's impotence as on his power. Indeed, the repetitions might themselves symbolise the artist's successive attempts to realise the ideal. In the fourth image, the sculptor perhaps attains his end; or perhaps not, for the two figures fail to make eye contact.

THE FLESHLY SCHOOL

Poetry and Scandal

As seen above (pp. 32–7), the paintings of the Rossetti circle could receive harsh notices when they appeared at public exhibition. However, the longer reviews of the circle's volumes of poetry generated more sustained controversies, and provided opportunities for critics to respond in detail to the circle's aesthetic ideas. All three of the Tudor House poets were attacked for immorality. George Meredith's *Modern Love*, a cycle of poems dealing with infidelity in marriage, raised critical eyebrows on its appearance in 1862. Swinburne's *Poems and Ballads* of 1866 elicited such outrage from critics that its original publisher withdrew it, fearing prosecution for obscenity or blasphemy; the volume was subsequently reissued by a publisher less particular about his reputation, John Camden Hotten. The shocked response to Swinburne's volume is scarcely surprising: one poem was

a passionate outburst in the character of Sappho, addressed to her female lover; others celebrated necrophilia; and four sonnets extolled the beauty of the classical statue of the Hermaphrodite in the Louvre. Some poems were overtly blasphemous; in 'Hymn to Proserpine' the speaker compares the austerity of the Virgin Mary unfavourably with the sensuality of the pagan love-goddess Venus.

Rossetti's own volume, *Poems* of 1870, was at first well received. Indeed, Rossetti had taken considerable trouble to organise sympathetic reviews in the major periodicals; notices by Swinburne, Morris, and other friends were predictably favourable. It was not until October 1871 that a violent attack appeared in the *Contemporary Review*, signed with a pseudonym, Thomas Maitland. In this case, the target was not Rossetti alone, but the entire circle – painters as well as poets, although the article was entitled 'The Fleshly School of Poetry'.

fig.44 D.G. Rossetti **The Sonnet** 1880
photograph of untraced pen-and-ink drawing, Delaware Art Museum,
Helen Farr Sloan Library Archives

At one level this was merely a personal vendetta; the author turned out to be Robert Buchanan, a young Scottish poet who had already crossed swords with both Swinburne and William Michael Rossetti. But his hostility is revealing. Buchanan, who was neither well-off nor well-connected, saw Rossetti and his friends as a privileged clique using their influence to support each other, and there was some justice to this view. On the other hand, the Rossetti circle had good reason to accuse Buchanan of cowardice in using a pseudonym. Amusingly, the publishers of the *Contemporary Review* wrote to the editor of the *Athenaeum* denying Buchanan's authorship at the same time as Buchanan himself wrote to acknowledge the article. The *Athenaeum* must have been delighted to expose this gaffe by publishing both letters in the same issue, along with a rejoinder by Rossetti himself, wittily entitled 'The Stealthy School of Criticism'.

The muddle over the pseudonym was inept; not so Buchanan's original article. The key word 'fleshly' was one that writers in Rossetti's circle had themselves been using to characterise the notion of an art of the senses; Swinburne had repeated it frequently in his descriptions of both pictures and poems by Rossetti. In the choice of this key word, and throughout his argument, Buchanan cleverly turned the circle's own terminology against itself. Buchanan summarised his main charges at the outset:

> the fleshly gentlemen have bound themselves
> by solemn league and covenant to extol fleshliness
> as the distinct and supreme end of poetic and
> pictorial art; to aver that poetic expression is
> greater than poetic thought, and by inference
> that the body is greater than the soul, and sound
> superior to sense; and that the poet, properly to
> develop his poetic faculty, must be an intellectual
> hermaphrodite, to whom the very facts of day and
> night are lost in a whirl of aesthetic terminology.

Both Swinburne's theoretical writings and Rossetti's poems indeed gave prominence to dichotomies such as body/soul,

sound/sense. Swinburne had in fact claimed that Rossetti's poems displayed an ideal union of the physical and spiritual, both in their treatment of romantic love as subject matter and in the technical balance of elegant rhyme and metre with meaningful content. Buchanan simply exaggerated the emphasis on the physical side in subject matter, and the technical side in versification, to present the whole project as an outrage on conventional morality.

Unacquainted with Rossetti's work in painting, Buchanan turned his ire on Simeon Solomon, ridiculing his pictures as 'pretty pieces of morality, such as "Love dying by the breath of Lust"'. No such picture by Solomon survives; perhaps Buchanan was making up a suitably shocking title. But he was probably thinking of works such as Solomon's *Love in Autumn* of 1866 (fig.45). The semi-nude youth, wings and drapery blown by harsh autumn winds, represents the fragility of love, echoed by the melancholy hues of the landscape, symbolic of the dying year. The pathos of the male figure suits the subject matter, but contradicted all contemporary conventions for the representation of masculinity. Buchanan rightly judged that the Rossetti circle was most vulnerable to the charge of undermining contemporary norms for vigorous masculinity, seen as central to British Imperial power and economic leadership. Throughout the article, he expertly deployed vocabulary suggesting effeminacy, as in the phrase 'intellectual hermaphrodite' quoted above.

Buchanan's attack was ill-tempered and prejudiced. But his unremitting denunciation of the sensual in art was at least consistent. Buchanan quoted Rossetti's sonnet 'Nuptial Sleep', which begins:

> At length their long kiss severed, with sweet
>   smart:
> And as the last slow sudden drops are shed
> From sparkling eaves when all the storm has
>   fled,
> So singly flagged the pulses of each heart.

fig.45 Simeon Solomon **Love in Autumn** 1866
oil on canvas 84 × 64 cm
Private Collection

It was scarcely unreasonable for Buchanan to interpret this as a representation of post-coital satiety. Rossetti's counter-argument, in 'The Stealthy School of Criticism', was that this poem was only one in a sequence of sonnets representing different aspects of love, with other poems stressing the spiritual to balance the emphasis on the sensual in this one. Rossetti might be accused of wanting it both ways – to write about sexual love yet to maintain a reputation for moral probity.

But Rossetti's response also points to serious questions about the circle's aesthetic project. Were they proposing a radical assault on contemporary morality, through frank treatment of sexuality and other contentious moral issues? Or were they proposing accommodation with contemporary moral notions through the claim that physical and spiritual love should be in harmony? Again, were they proposing a radical elevation of artistic form at the expense of moral content, or merely an increased attention to form in the interests of artistic excellence?

As suggested above, the members of the circle were experimenting with all of these options. Swinburne's *William Blake* tended to favour the most radical of them. Rossetti's 'Stealthy School' was more moderate, no doubt partly because the circumstances required him to appear more temperate than Buchanan. But there is no reason to accuse Rossetti of equivocation. The issues about art and morality, form and content were too complex to admit a neat solution. They were explored in a wide variety of different ways, not only in writing, but in the art of Rossetti and his friends.

fig.46 D.G. Rossetti **Study for The Blessed Damozel** 1876
crayon and chalk on paper 39.9 × 93 cm
Harvard University Art Museums (Fogg Art Museum), Cambridge, Massachusetts, Bequest of Grenville L. Winthrop

fig.47 G.F. Watts **A Study with the Peacock's Feathers** 1862–5
oil on panel 66 × 56 cm
Pre-Raphaelite Inc. by courtesy of Julian Hartnoll

fig.48 D.G. Rossetti **Venus Verticordia** 1864–8
oil on canvas 70 × 82.5 cm
Russell-Cotes Art Gallery and Museum, Bournemouth

The Nude

Had Buchanan known more about Rossetti's friendships among painters, he would have been able to fortify his attack. Beginning in the later 1860s, the painters of both Rossetti's circle and the interlocking Holland Park circle devoted their attention to the 'fleshly' in the most literal sense: with a striking revival of the painting of the nude figure, both male and female. Since the nude had been exceedingly inconspicuous in British art since the death of William Etty in 1849, the revival could not have been a more dramatic event; its ramifications have been explored at length in a recent book on the Victorian nude by the art historian Alison Smith. The artists of the Holland Park circle led the way in reintroducing the nude at public exhibition; Watts, Leighton, and Albert Moore all contributed major paintings of the nude to the Royal Academy exhibitions between 1866 and 1869. At exactly the same time, Whistler, Rossetti, and Burne-Jones experimented with the representation of the nude figure, although Whistler failed to complete his projected pictures of *Venus Rising from the Sea* (two unfinished oils are now in the Freer Gallery of Art, Washington, D.C.). This was clearly a project that was shared between the two circles.

One of the subtlest explorations of the sensuality of the female nude is Watts's *A Study with the Peacock's Feathers* (fig.47). Like the same artist's *The Wife of Pygmalion* (fig.39), the half-length format recalls Rossetti's work. So too the remoteness of the gaze and the languour of the pose, suggesting as in Rossetti's pictures an erotic self-absorption. The pale figure is far less earthy than Rossetti's female figures of the 1860s, but the sense of her physical perfection does not diminish the sensual appeal: the raised arm reveals a perfectly hairless underarm, with the gentlest of modelling to indicate the swelling of the breasts, and crumpled white drapery to contrast with the smoothness of the flesh. The few talismanic accessories, amber beads and peacock feather, also emphasise the seamless perfection of the smooth nude flesh by contrast.

Very different is Rossetti's *Venus Verticordia* (fig.48), despite the similar format of half-length figure with accessories to contrast with the naked flesh. Altogether more strident than the subtle tones of Watts's accessories is the lush profusion of Rossetti's flowers: the roses behind the figure are emblematic of love, and the vivid honeysuckle is an even more obvious visual symbol for the figure's sexuality. Indeed, Rossetti's old friend John Ruskin took particular exception to the flowers, perhaps displacing his uneasiness about the sensuality of the figure. In a letter to Rossetti, he wrote that the flowers 'were wonderful to me, in their realism; awful – I can use no other word – in their coarseness'. Rossetti also includes more traditional symbolism: the dart of love pointing toward the exposed breast, the apple of temptation, and the butterflies, symbols of souls, perhaps of men enthralled by the goddess of beauty. More curious is what appears to be a radiant halo behind the figure's head – an inappropriate symbol to confer on a pagan goddess, but recalling Swinburne's blasphemous elevation of the pagan Venus above the Virgin Mary. Later writers often described Rossetti's pictures of women as establishing a religion of beauty; here the hint of an iconic function is particularly strong. But it is unclear whether the worship of Venus is holy or occult. The 'Verticordia' of the title means 'turning hearts'. But does that imply turning the heart toward the beloved – or away from another?

The depiction of Venus, the classical goddess of beauty, neatly fulfilled the demand for aesthetic purity in subject matter. Accordingly, a high proportion of pictures of the female nude had Venus as subject; in addition to the Rossetti, there were the two unfinished versions by Whistler, and Royal Academy pictures of Venus by both Leighton in 1867, and Albert Moore in 1869, later joined by many others. The subject had additional claim to pure art status, since Venus had been the favourite subject for paintings of the female nude throughout the history of art, from Titian's *Venus of Urbino* to Ingres's *Venus Anadyomene*, to name only two examples that were particularly admired in the Rossetti and Holland Park circles.

Burne-Jones chose a more obscure classical myth for his essay in the nude, *Phyllis and Demophoön* (fig.49), which was hung at the Old Water-Colour Society exhibition of 1870 but removed almost immediately; this was the only example of a scandal in painting equivalent to the scandals over the circle's poetry. Although Leighton had exhibited a picture with a male nude at the Royal Academy the previous year, *Daedalus and Icarus* (Faringdon Collection, Buscot Park), the figure had been provided with a wisp of drapery; Burne-Jones's Demophoön was the first male figure to appear totally nude. Complaints at the private view led to a request to withdraw the watercolour; Burne-Jones complied, but also resigned from the Society, thus losing the principal public forum for his painting. The interpretation of the subject may have added to the difficulty. In the ancient legend, Phyllis, daughter of the king of Thrace, had been changed into an almond tree after her death from grief after the departure of her faithless lover, Demophoön; returning later, the remorseful Demophoön embraced the tree, which blossomed as a token of forgiveness and continuing love. The watercolour virtually reverses the legend's roles for the male and female figures: it is Phyllis, half-transformed back into human form, who reaches to embrace a Demophoön whose gesture suggests a wish to flee. Although her legs remain imprisoned within the tree, the female figure is the more active, the male more passive. The nudity of the male figure perhaps made him appear vulnerable, although the body is more muscular and virile than the nude youth in Solomon's *Love in Autumn* (fig.45). Moreover, the faces of the two figures, like those of Pygmalion and his statue, resemble each other uncannily. The watercolour was at least as much an assault on conventional notions of masculinity as it was a challenge to prudishness.

fig.49 Edward Burne-Jones **Phyllis and Demophoön** 1870
opaque watercolour 91.5 × 45.8 cm

Birmingham Museums and Art Gallery

THE GROSVENOR GALLERY

The Circle in the 1870s

In the early 1870s the Rossetti and Holland Park circles lost cohesion; the days of concerted enterprise were apparently over. This might be attributed to the series of débacles that began with the scandal over *Phyllis and Demophoön*; in quick succession came the 'Fleshly School' controversy, Rossetti's nervous breakdown, and Solomon's arrest. The artists had good reason to draw back and regroup, after the period of experimentation in the 1860s.

But the traditional ending of the Bohemian myth also played a part; in Murger's novel and the many English articles on the subject, Bohemianism was a phase in an archetypal life cycle, ending with the artists' maturity, integration into society, and worldly prosperity. By the time of the 'Fleshly School' controversy Rossetti was forty-three, Burne-Jones thirty-eight; they were selling their works to a circle of faithful patrons at steadily increasing prices. The artists of the Holland Park circle were more successful still; Watts and Leighton had been elected Royal Academicians in 1867 and 1868 respectively.

Unlike the Holland Park artists, those closest to Rossetti continued to hold aloof from the Royal Academy, still the ultimate symbol of artistic respectability. After Burne-Jones's resignation from the Old Water-Colour Society, he showed occasionally at the Dudley Gallery as did Whistler and the younger followers of the circle. But there was an increasing perception within the art world that a significant section of the British school lacked an appropriate forum for their work.

It was partly in response to this perception that the amateur artist and minor aristocrat, Sir Coutts Lindsay, formed the plan of opening the Grosvenor Gallery – no Bohemian venture, but a major new exhibiting institution, with a grand and costly building in New Bond Street (fig.50), considerable social cachet, and an elite selection of exhibitors, hand-picked by Lindsay. This curious mixture of aesthetic elitism, high-society glamour, and commercial opportunism was an instant success: seven thousand visitors thronged to the first day of the first exhibition in 1877, which was reviewed prominently in all the major periodicals.

The list of exhibitors invited by Lindsay was very different from the miscellany of the Royal Academy, but nonetheless diverse. The Grosvenor Gallery gave exhibition space to a number of groups thought to be inadequately represented at the Academy, including women artists, watercolour painters, amateurs, and foreign artists. But the most conspicuous exhibitors, judging by press commentary, were those of the Rossetti and Holland Park groups, with their extended circles of followers. Virtually all of the artists mentioned above were present: Whistler and Burne-Jones, Watts and Leighton, Crane and Bateman, along with a host of tangential associates of the circles, and more recent followers.

fig.50 **Intended facade of the Grosvenor Gallery, New Bond Street** *The Builder* 5 May 1877, p. 453
line engraving

No one remarked on the absence of Solomon, whose name had become unmentionable since his arrest in 1873. But the other significant absence was well publicised: that of Rossetti, who even wrote to the editor of *The Times* to explain the reasons for his non-participation. The publication of Rossetti's letter in that august newspaper was tantamount to proof of success for his strategy of invisible mystique. Rossetti adopted a tone of high-minded humility: 'What holds me back is simply the lifelong feeling of dissatisfaction which I have experienced from the disparity of aim and attainment in what I have all my life produced as best I could'. But the letter ensured the noteworthiness of his absence, a symbol of the purity of his dedication to his art. Moreover, Rossetti took care to alert the public to his leadership of an important artistic movement, by recommending attention to his disciple: the Grosvenor Gallery 'must succeed', he wrote, 'were it but for one name associated with it – that of Burne-Jones – a name representing the loveliest art we have'.

The Grosvenor Gallery exhibitions, from 1877 onward, thus marked the graduation of the entire circle from Bohemian separatism to participation in the public sphere. Not all critics approved. The charges of effeminacy, eccentricity, and morbidity recurred frequently, particularly against Burne-Jones. But if doubts persisted about the healthiness or normalcy of the circle's art, its importance could no longer be denied.

Watts and Burne-Jones at the Grosvenor

One mark of significance was literal indeed: the vast size of the Grosvenor pictures of Watts, Burne-Jones, Crane, and many of the others. The Rossettian half-length of the 1860s had rarely exceeded dimensions of three by three feet. But major Grosvenor exhibits were often well over eight feet high, covering a surface area four or five times that of the earlier pictures. That changed their impact in the most dramatic way: now the pictures were larger than the human beings who contemplated them.

Watts had exhibited a first version of his composition, *Love and Death*, at the Dudley Gallery in 1870; at five by two-and-a-half feet, it was a large picture for its date (Bristol City Museum and Art Gallery). But the version of the same composition that appeared at the first Grosvenor Gallery exhibition measured more than eight feet by four (fig.51). The increased dimensions meant that the forbidding figure of Death, heavily draped and faceless, was now larger than life in physical as well as concepual terms.

Watts's subject was an allegory, according to traditional terminology; the word derives from the Greek for 'other', implying that what was depicted stood for something 'other than' itself. Thus, the nude boy represented the concept of Love, the draped adult that of Death. But Watts's own term for his compositions of this sort was 'symbolical'. In the terms of current theoretical debate on the merits of the symbolic, versus the allegorical, Watts's terminology implies a denial that his depiction was something 'other than' its meaning. By implication, the picture should be experienced *as* Love and Death, not intellectualised as a mere allegory of Love and Death.

The composition is strange, by any traditional rules: a figure with its back turned dominates the picture space and casts a heavy shadow on the other figure, forced into a tight space on one side of an unconventionally elongated vertical format. But the dynamic alternation of sharp diagonals within the constricted upright space makes its impact; the small figure of Love tilts backward in vulnerability, extending

fig.51 G.F. Watts **Love and Death** c.1874–7
oil on canvas 248.9 × 116.8 cm
The Whitworth Art Gallery, University of Manchester

an arm in ineffectual self-protection as the colossal veiled figure stretches a more powerful arm in a dramatically fore-shortened gesture of victory. Death's inexorability is the more terrifying since the face is unseen. For Oscar Wilde, reviewing the first Grosvenor Gallery exhibition, this succeeded in making the spectator feel the scene as lived experience: 'we can see from the terror in the boy's eyes and quivering lips, that, Medusa-like, this grey phantom turns all it looks upon to stone; and the wings of Love are rent and crushed'. Watts draws on traditional symbols for the figure of Love – not only his wings, but the roses and dove, forlorn in the lower right corner. But Death has no attributes; even its gender is uncertain. The massive grandeur of the form and the heavy drapery folds, as if deeply cut in stone, epitomise rather than allegorise the idea.

Watts repeated this powerful composition on a number of canvases of varying sizes; in other works, for which the Grosvenor was the principal public forum, he gave physical form to equally abstract ideas on equally vast canvases. But Burne-Jones was not to be outscaled; he too began to work with dimensions that made his earlier work Lilliputian by contrast. And Rossetti's forecast proved correct; after years of near-invisibility, Burne-Jones's work suddenly became the centre of attention at the Grosvenor. According to Burne-Jones's wife, the opening of the Grosvenor changed the artist's public profile irrevocably: 'From that day he belonged to the world in a sense that he had never done before, for his existence became widely known and his name famous'. As the novelist and critic Henry James remarked in 1882, 'A Grosvenor without Mr. Burne-Jones is a Hamlet with Hamlet left out'.

If Watts represented the Grosvenor Gallery Sublime, Burne-Jones's work might be called the Grosvenor Gallery Beautiful. *The Golden Stairs* (fig.52), exhibited in 1880, used an exaggerated vertical format nearly nine feet high to convey an effect virtually opposite to Watts's massiveness; the serpentine staircase winds up the picture surface with little hint of spatial depth, as a host of near-identical maidens descend, their perfect feet barely touching the steps.

'Maidens' they are always called; all trace of Rossettian earthiness seems to have been refined away along with the dense textures and rich colouring of the 1860s watercolours, to leave a tonality barely ranging between blond and silvery, and bodies that seem exempt from the law of gravity. The sense of endless circling in a space that leads nowhere sets up a timelessness where the maidens are perpetual virgins, to be forever desired and never possessed. This has its own erotic charge, but one very different from the Rossettian types of earlier decades. The musical theme, too, seems etherealised; the rhythms of the lines and the harmonies of the colours suggest a fainter, more distant music than the powerful sensuous impact proposed in many musical subjects of the 1860s.

The Golden Stairs is easy to relate to the common view of Burne-Jones's work as a pessimistic form of escapism, presenting a utopia of pure beauty and harmony that can never be attained. A statement of the artist's has often been quoted:

> I mean by a picture a beautiful romantic dream
> of something that never was, never will be –
> in a light better than any light that ever shone –
> in a land no one can define, or remember, only
> desire…

The apparent defeatism of this view has been contrasted with the belief of Burne-Jones's lifelong friend, William Morris, in political action aimed at making utopia a social reality. Indeed, it might be argued that Burne-Jones's pictures were anti-activist. By satisfying spectators' imaginations with dreams of beauty, they dulled the urge to take action for social change. On the other hand, the pictures might be seen as a form of protest against contemporary social reality, criticising the real world by symbolising one more beautiful.

Exhibition at the Grosvenor Gallery might seem to sully the image's purity, either as social comment or as art. By exhibiting at the Grosvenor, artists such as Watts and Burne-Jones bolstered their reputations as elite painters; prices

fig.52 Edward Burne-Jones **The Golden Stairs** 1880
oil on canvas 269.2 × 116.8 cm
Tate Gallery

fig.53 George Du Maurier **Ye Aesthetic Young Geniuses**
Punch, 21 September 1878, p.122

skyrocketed, and mystical paintings with recondite 'symbolical' meanings moved from the realm of artistic experimentation into that of fashion. Satire followed fashionability; George Du Maurier's *Punch* cartoon of 1878 pokes fun at a coterie of affectedly Bohemian artists (fig.53), and Gilbert and Sullivan's operetta *Patience* satirised the 'greenery yallery Grosvenor Gallery'. However, ridicule would have been pointless if the art of the Grosvenor Gallery had not been successful. The publicity and prosperity that attended the Grosvenor perhaps marks the end of Bohemian idealism, but the alternative would have been perpetual obscurity for the art of the circle. As Murger himself had pointed out, the Bohemian artist who does not succeed to recognition and acceptability is doomed to oblivion.

Whistler versus Ruskin

By 1877 Whistler's work had moved away from that of his former friends in the Rossetti circle. His *Nocturnes* might, nonetheless, be described as escapist, representing the banks of the Thames but mystifying all signs of industry and social reality in nocturnal shadow and swathes of mist. The ethereal veils of colour Whistler was using had their origin in the shared experiments in colour harmony of the 1860s; Burne-Jones's *Green Summer* (fig.27) restricts the palette in much the same way as Whistler's *Nocturne in Blue and Silver* (fig.54). But Whistler's sketchy touch had diverged so far from Burne-Jones's precision of handling, by 1877, that no critic attempted to compare them.

One critic, however, pitted them against each other in a fashion that was to bring the aesthetic debates of the circle into public as never before. John Ruskin, after an extravagant eulogy of Burne-Jones's work, attacked Whistler's paintings in the strongest language:

> For Mr. Whistler's own sake, no less than for the protection of the purchaser, Sir Coutts Lindsay ought not to have admitted works into the gallery in which the ill-educated conceit of the artist so nearly approached the aspect of wilful imposture. I have seen, and heard, much of Cockney impudence before now; but never expected to hear a coxcomb ask two hundred guineas for flinging a pot of paint in the public's face.

Whistler decided to sue Ruskin for libel. The resulting courtroom drama has usually been presented as a battle between art for art's sake and a Philistine subjection of art to moral and realistic purposes; indeed, that view of the trial made it famous among the continental Symbolists. But a glance at the cast of characters in the courtroom suggests a more complex story. Among the witnesses on Whistler's side were William Michael Rossetti and Albert Moore; on Ruskin's side was Burne-Jones. The testimony, recently reconstructed

fig.54 J.A.M. Whistler **Nocturne in Blue and Silver: Cremorne Lights** 1872
oil on canvas 50.2 × 74.3 cm
Tate Gallery

from contemporary newspaper reports by Linda Merrill, shows that the issues of the 1860s were still alive.

When Whistler was asked to explain the title, *Nocturne*, given to his night-time landscapes, he answered:

> By using the word 'nocturne' I wished to indicate an artistic interest alone, divesting the picture of any outside anecdotal interest which might have been otherwise attached to it. A nocturne is an arrangement of line, form, and colour first.

Whistler recommends the non-symbolising symbol; he maintains that the visible forms of the picture need make no symbolic reference to ideas beyond themselves. Moreover, he goes on to deny that the musical connotation of the word 'nocturne' (recalling the piano pieces by Chopin) implied any reference to further meanings for the pictures:

> Among my works are some night pieces, and I have chosen the word 'nocturne' because it generalizes and simplifies the whole set of them; it is an accident that I happened upon terms used in music. Very often have I been misunderstood from this fact, it having been supposed that I intended some way or other to show a connection between the two arts, whereas I had no such intention.

Whistler was surely being disingenuous. He had begun to use musical titles for his pictures in the later 1860s, when he was still in close social contact with Rossetti and the other artists who were exploring the notion of synaesthetic correspondences between paintings and music. Nonetheless, the extreme position he adopts, refusing all symbolic meaning for the visible forms in his pictures, derives from the shared explorations of the 1860s among the members of the Rossetti and Holland Park circles.

Even in 1877, Whistler was still pitting the notion of the non-symbolising symbol against its opposite, the possibility of proliferating meaning. When questioned about what was represented in his pictures, he kept both possibilities in play. The judge asked whether *Nocturne in Blue and Silver* was 'a correct representation of Battersea Bridge'. Whistler answered: 'As to what the picture represents, that depends upon who looks at it'. When asked whether the shapes on the bridge represented people, Whistler answered: 'They are just what you like'. These answers acknowledge another strand in the Rossetti group's thinking – the possibility that the visible symbols on the canvas do not refer to one specific meaning, but may lead the spectator's imagination in any number of different directions; the possibility, in short, of the proliferating symbol.

Little wonder that Burne-Jones's testimony, later in the trial, seems to equivocate. As a witness for Ruskin his role was to oppose Whistler, but the aesthetic views Whistler expressed were versions of those Burne-Jones himself was still exploring. Burne-Jones could not bring himself to repudiate Whistler's experiments in colour harmonies; at the

AN APPEAL TO THE LAW.
NAUGHTY CRITIC, TO USE BAD LANGUAGE! SILLY PAINTER, TO GO TO LAW ABOUT IT!

fig.55 Linley Sambourne **Whistler Versus Ruskin**
Punch, 7 December 1878, p.254

time of the trial he had already begun work on *The Golden Stairs* (fig.52), which might just as well be titled *Arrangement in Blue and Gold*. He was therefore obliged to concentrate on the issue of finish, certainly the area in which Whistler's work had diverged furthest from the practice of Rossetti and Burne-Jones.

Later in Burne-Jones's testimony another issue emerged. Ruskin's counsel produced a picture attributed to Titian as an example of a completely finished picture to contrast with Whistler's sketchy works. Asked to describe the Venetian painting, Burne-Jones cleverly twisted Whistler's own words from earlier in the trial, declaring it an 'arrangement in flesh and blood'. The phrase hints at one interpretation of the notion of an art of the senses, as one redolent with human life and passion. By contrast, Whistler's phrase 'arrangement of line, form, and colour first' suggests a more austere ideal of formal perfection, one that accorded well with the art of one of Whistler's main witnesses, Albert Moore (fig.35). The two phrases mark a fundamental difference of opinion among the artists, one that may have been under debate since the 1860s. Moreover, they represent shades of opinion on the basic question of the relationship between visible form and connoted meaning; Burne-Jones was unwilling to relinquish the notion that the painted forms might have important human significance. Whistler endorses the notion of the non-symbolising symbol; Burne-Jones inclines towards that of the proliferating symbol.

That difference of opinion passed unnoticed by the many newspaper correspondents who reported on the trial, briefly a topic of public notoriety at the end of 1878. Linley Sambourne's cartoon for *Punch* (fig.55) satirises the outcome of the trial, showing a bewigged judge awarding the verdict to Whistler, but offering him only a derisory farthing in damages. Whistler's victory was scarcely a resounding one, and perhaps appropriately so; the aesthetic issues raised at the trial could not be resolved by the legal system. Indeed, the court's refusal to deliver a clear judgment marked a victory for the circle's aesthetic programme at its broadest. The meanings of a work of art could not be determined, one way or another, in a legally binding way.

TOWARD SYMBOLISM

Interpreting Rossetti

Throughout the public discussions of the Grosvenor Gallery and the Whistler-Ruskin trial, Rossetti remained in self-imposed isolation at Tudor House. A drawing by Frederic Shields (fig.56), one of the younger men who continued to flock around Rossetti, shows him in 1880, no longer youthfully slender but still engaged in his most character-istic pursuit, painting a picture of a woman (*The Day Dream*, Victoria and Albert Museum, London). As the draw

ing suggests, Rossetti too was now working at increased dimensions. *Astarte Syriaca* (fig.57), seen by many friends and associates as the great picture of his later years, presents a figure at three-quarter length on a canvas six feet high. The subject is the Syrian goddess of love, described in the accompanying sonnet as more ancient still than the classical Venus; to his associates, Rossetti seemed to be searching back through the ages for the originating symbol of the idea he was perpetually struggling to embody. For William Michael Rossetti, the painting at last resolved the dichotomy in Rossetti's character as well as his art: 'he had aimed to make it equally strong in abstract sentiment and in physical grandeur'. Indeed, William Michael described the painting as uniting the meanings of *Lady Lilith* and *Sibylla Palmifera*.

Those remarks occur in William Michael's volume of 1889, *Dante Gabriel Rossetti as Designer and Writer*, one of many books and articles that suddenly revealed the artist to the public after his death in 1882. At last Rossetti's pictures appeared at public exhibition, beginning with the memorial exhibitions held at the Burlington Fine Arts Club and the Royal Academy – the latter a remarkable event, as critics noted, since no picture by Rossetti had ever graced the Academy's walls during his lifetime. The situation was the stuff of romance, and it was greeted with enthusiasm by the press.

Attention centred, inevitably, on the Rossetti female type; debate raged about whether Rossetti had simply repeated himself with ever-increasing mannerism, or whether he had indeed created an original image of female beauty. *Punch* satirised the Rossetti woman, playing on the charges of repetitiveness, enervation, and morbidity that had been levelled against the circle for decades:

fig.56 Frederic Shields **Rossetti Working on 'The Day Dream'**
1880 pencil on paper 18.4 × 11.8 cm, Ashmolean Museum, Oxford

fig.57 D.G. Rossetti **Astarte Syriaca** 1875–7
oil on canvas 182.8 × 106.5 cm
Manchester City Art Galleries

Nearly all the women here have got auburn wigs, apparently misfits from a theatrical perruquier, bought second-hand. And nearly all are more or less sea-sickly, 'greenery-yallery' young women, natives of one of the States of Indigestion. Never saw such lackadaisical floppers as the sea-sickly women; but take the lot, they're all either unwholesome or unhealthy.

Other critics, notably those who were friends or relatives (in the case of William Michael), gave a more positive view. Rossetti's former Pre-Raphaelite Brother F.G. Stephens subtly protected Rossetti's personal reputation, with interpretations of the pictures that muted the sensual elements to stress the spiritual.

The art critic Sidney Colvin had been a tangential associate of the circle and a particular champion of Burne-Jones since the later 1860s. Now Slade Professor at Cambridge and Director of the Fitzwilliam Museum, he elegantly recapitulated the familiar theme of the two sides of Rossetti's art:

> Either he simply takes some type of beauty that interests him, attires her in gorgeous and far-fetched ornaments, and strains all his powers to express as he feels it the mere sensuous charm of womanhood and rich array: or else he invests her with a halo of intellectual attributes and secondary meanings, making of herself a personification, and a symbol of everything that adorns her.

This draws on the major themes present since the 1860s: the division between the sensuous and spiritual sides of art, and the corresponding division between an art that refuses to symbolise and one that gives out symbolic suggestions to infinity.

On the Continent

Rossetti's memorial exhibitions were also reviewed in France, where his name had been known since the 1860s, but his works unseen, as in England. Théodore Duret, writing in the *Gazette des Beaux-Arts*, saw Rossetti's work in utter contrast to the 'utilitarian and puritanical' tendencies of English culture. Whether one loved or loathed his work, Duret thought, its originality had to be acknowledged. Like English critics, Duret concentrated on the Rossetti woman:

> a colossal being, having on a large neck a head strongly accentuated, with salient lips and an enormous head of luxuriant hair. This creature, a kind of sibyl, siren, or melusine, has none of the delicate graces of woman; she is nonetheless very living and, when one has gazed at her for some time, she becomes unforgettable; she exercises a kind of fascination, but mixed with inquietude; one is afraid to come too close to her, one fears that if she took you by the arms, she would make your bones crack.

Note Duret's shift from the impersonal pronoun 'one' to the urgent 'you': the sentence makes the reader feel the impact of the image. Duret's interpretation of the Rossetti woman as an image of terror was more extreme than any English view of the artist's work. In France the art of Rossetti and his circle was seen at a slight distance, as an exotic phenomenon; the emphasis was on the wierd, the unfathomable, the sinister.

Rossetti's art, mostly confined to private collections, remained difficult to see, but French audiences were able to see much of Watts and Burne-Jones, who showed at the great Universal Exhibitions held in Paris in 1878 and 1889. As their French reputations grew, both artists were also welcomed at the major French annual exhibitions, the Salons, and at smaller shows in Paris. Their work made a special

D.G. Rossetti **Astarte Syriaca** 1875–7 (detail of fig.57

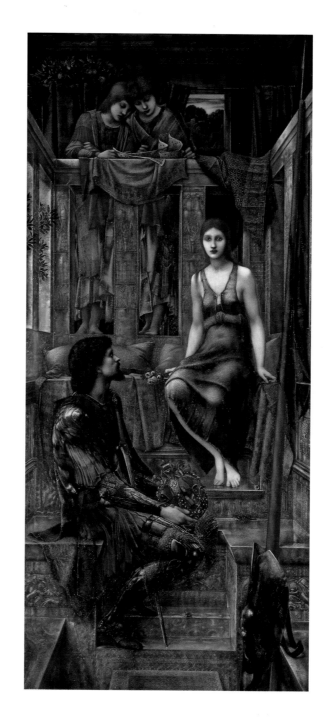

fig.58 Edward Burne-Jones **King Cophetua and the Beggar Maid** 1884
oil on canvas 293.4 × 135.9 cm

impact on the writers who were beginning to be designated Symbolists. As in the case of Rossetti, though, the French writers tended to emphasise different aspects of the work from those discussed in English exhibition reviews.

For instance, the characterisation of Watts's art in Joris-Karl Huysmans's famous novel, *A rebours* (*Against Nature*, 1884) would no doubt have horrified the painter, but reveals the fascination Watts's pictures could have on a foreign audience to whom they were unfamiliar. Huysmans transforms Watts's allegories from meditations on the mysteries of human existence to bizarre symbols of decadence:

> paintings designed by an ailing Gustave Moreau, brushed by an anaemic Michelangelo and retouched by a Raphael drowned in blue… in the singular and mysterious amalgam of these three masters emerges the personality at once over-refined and primitive of an Englishman scholarly and a dreamer, tormented by obsessions and unbearable tints.

In the writings of Huysmans and others, the English artists were linked to French artists who were also being taken up as precursors of Symbolism – Gustave Moreau, Odilon Redon, Puvis de Chavannes.

Burne-Jones made a dramatic impact at the Paris Exposition Universelle of 1889, where his sole exhibit was *King Cophetua and the Beggar Maid* (fig.58), first seen at the Grosvenor Gallery in 1884. The story, drawn from an old English ballad that Tennyson had also used for a poem, tells of a king who falls in love with a beggar; in the picture the king removes his crown, symbol of his power and wealth, to gaze at the humble woman. Her elevation above the king could be read as reversing their social classes, or proclaiming a spiritual value that transcends both political and economic power. However, the French critic Robert de la Sizeranne described the subject more precisely as 'the symbolical expression of the Scorn of Wealth'. For the French critic, its appearance at the Exposition Universelle,

dedicated to the display of the wealth of the modern industrialised nations, marked a kind of protest; it appeared a political fable rather than an escapist fantasy, as English commentators have characterised it. The image might be read as marking contemporary tensions within itself: the beauty of the beggar maid in her simple shift, just slightly tattered at the edges, competes for the spectator's attention with the material splendour of the surroundings.

The French reception of Burne-Jones, Watts, and Rossetti drew out certain aspects of the works, less emphasised in England – danger, terror, and decadence. The English pictures made a powerful impact also on the Belgian Symbolists. For example, Fernand Khnopff, a passionate admirer of Burne-Jones, pays homage also to Rossetti in *I Lock my Door upon Myself* (fig.59). The title quotes a poem by Rossetti's sister Christina, while Khnopff's picture represents a figure modelled by his own sister in a closed room full of talismanic artefacts. Khnopff emphasises the enigmatic or mystical aspects seen in the work of Rossetti and his circle by continental observers.

Rossetti and the Religion of Beauty

The interpretation of the Rossetti circle's painting by the continental Symbolists might be said to make mysterious an art which English critics tended increasingly to sanitise. More recently the art has perhaps been debased, through endless repetition in calendars and greetings cards. But each kind of response brings out an aspect of the images. Even the trivialising reproductions might be said to respond to the urge toward repetition, a conspicuous aspect of the original images. No single interpretation of the art of Rossetti and his associates is adequate; in that sense the works are indeed proliferating symbols.

In an essay published in 1883, the classical scholar F.W.H. Myers offered perhaps the most erudite version of the body-and-soul theme that continued to dominate accounts of Rossetti's work. He interpreted Rossetti's art in the light of Plato's philosophy, presenting the paintings as sensuous images of transcendent Platonic Ideas, leading the spectator on a spiritual journey from the 'fleshly' through beauty to contemplation of the divine. Myers characterised Rossetti's pictures of women as 'the sacred pictures of a new religion'. This subtle interpretation is anchored not only in classical philosophy, but in the contemporary social context; Myers argues that the pictures reflect the rising status of women in the contemporary world. Moreover, he seeks in Rossetti's art an image of salvation to heal an age of religious doubt.

Myers responds to the sense, implicit in many discussions of Rossetti's work, that the pictures are latter-day cult images.

The title of Myers's article, 'Rossetti and the Religion of Beauty', caught on, and not without reason. The repetitive character of the images is perhaps their salient feature, multiplied through the repetition of the Rossettian type in the work of other artists. Myers finds a positive justification, by attributing a function akin to Byzantine icons, religious images that are equally repetitive.

Rossetti's art might then be seen as yearning for the recovery of art's social function in pre-modern societies, as cult image. But the repetitive character of the pictures also alludes to the nineteenth-century commodification of art so often lamented by contemporaries. The pictures' repetitiveness thus hovers between acknowledgement of the commercial status of art in the modern world, and longing for a return to the cult function of earlier ages. In that sense, the art of the Rossetti circle might be described as a form of protest through capitulation, one that acknowledges the mass-produced nature of the modern work of art while simultaneously alluding to its lost iconic function.

That is an interpretation for our age. The images have become calendar art; to pretend otherwise would be futile. Yet their mystique refuses to dissipate. We experience them both as endlessly reproducible commercial products and as uniquely compelling works of art.

fig.59 Fernand Khnopff **I Lock My Door Upon Myself** 1891
oil on canvas 72 × 140 cm

Neue Pinakothek, Munich

fig.60 D.G. Rossetti **Monna Vanna** 1866
oil on canvas 88.9 × 86.4 cm
Tate Gallery

CHRONOLOGY

1817
George Frederic Watts born

1828
Dante Gabriel Rossetti born

1829
William Michael Rossetti, Frederick Sandys, and Elizabeth Siddall born

1830
Frederic Leighton and Christina Georgina Rossetti born

1833
Edward Burne-Jones born

1834
William Morris and James McNeill Whistler born

1837
Algernon Charles Swinburne born
Queen Victoria ascends the throne

1840
Simeon Solomon born

1848
Pre-Raphaelite Brotherhood formed in September with seven members: Dante Gabriel and William Michael Rossetti, the sculptor Thomas Woolner, and the painters James Collinson, William Holman Hunt, John Everett Millais, and Frederic George Stephens (later a major art critic)

1849
First public exhibitions of paintings by the Pre-Raphaelite Brotherhood, at the Royal Academy (Millais and Hunt) and the Free Exhibition (Rossetti's *The Girlhood of Mary Virgin*)
Elizabeth Siddall introduced to Pre-Raphaelite circle

1850
Harsh press notices of Pre-Raphaelite paintings, including Rossetti's *Ecce Ancilla Domini* at the National Exhibition, his second and last submission to the annual London exhibitions of contemporary painting
Watts moves to Little Holland House as guest of the Prinseps

1851
Great Exhibition in the Crystal Palace, Hyde Park, initiating series of international exhibitions of fine and industrial arts in European capitals

1853
Burne-Jones and Morris meet as Oxford undergraduates

1855
Exposition Universelle, the first international exhibition to include painting, held in Paris
Frederic Leighton's first Royal Academy painting, *Cimabue's Madonna*, attracts acclaim

1857
Mural decoration project at the Oxford Union Society organised by Rossetti, including works by Burne-Jones and Morris; Oxford associates include Swinburne and Jane Burden (1839–1913)

1859
Rossetti paints *Bocca Baciata*
Morris and Burden marry
Leighton and Whistler settle in London

1860
Rossetti and Siddall marry

1861
Rossetti publishes *The Early Italian Poets*

1862
Siddall dies in February
Rossetti moves in the autumn to Tudor House, Cheyne Walk, Chelsea, where his lodgers include his brother William Michael, Swinburne, and George Meredith, whose controversial volume of poetry, *Modern Love*, is published the same year
Whistler is introduced to the Rossetti circle

1864
Burne-Jones elected Associate of the Old Water-Colour Society
Leighton elected Associate of the Royal Academy, and begins to build a studio house near Little Holland House

1865
Burne-Jones's exhibits at the Old Water-Colour Society attract attention of Walter Crane and other young painters

1866
Swinburne's *Poems and Ballads* published and immediately withdrawn by Edward Moxon & Co.; reissued by John Camden Hotten
Sandys lodges with Rossetti at Tudor House

1867
Watts elected Royal Academician

1868
Swinburne publishes *William Blake* and *Notes on the Royal Academy Exhibition* (with William Michael Rossetti)
Leighton elected Royal Academician

1870
Burne-Jones resigns from Old Water-Colour Society after controversy about *Phyllis and Demophoön*
Rossetti publishes *Poems*

1871
Robert Buchanan publishes 'The Fleshly School of Poetry', attacking Rossetti and his associates, in the *Contemporary Review*

1872
Rossetti suffers a nervous breakdown

1873
Solomon arrested and convicted for homosexual offences

1877
First exhibition of the Grosvenor Gallery, with major successes for Burne-Jones and Watts; Rossetti refuses to exhibit but completes *Astarte Syriaca*

1878
Whistler sues John Ruskin for libel and wins a farthing in damages
Exposition Universelle, Paris, brings Continental fame to Watts and Burne-Jones
Leighton elected President of the Royal Academy

1882
Rossetti dies; memorial exhibitions in the winter of 1882–3 at the Royal Academy and Burlington Fine Arts Club reveal his work, previously little known in public

1886
Symbolist manifestoes published in French periodicals

1889
Exposition Universelle held in Paris, with special acclaim for Burne-Jones's King *Cophetua and the Beggar Maid*

1894
Christina Rossetti dies

1896
Leighton and Morris die

1898
Burne-Jones dies

1901
Queen Victoria dies and is succeeded by Edward VII

1903
Whistler dies

1904
Sandys and Watts die

1905
Solomon dies

1909
Swinburne dies

1919
William Michael Rossetti dies

Selected Bibliography

Virginia M. Allen, ' "One Strangling Golden Hair": Dante Gabriel Rossetti's *Lady Lilith*', *Art Bulletin*, vol.66, 1984, pp. 285–94.

Mrs Russell Barrington, *The Life, Letters and Work of Frederic Leighton*, London 1906, 2 vols.

Robert Buchanan (signed with pseudonym Thomas Maitland), 'The Fleshly School of Poetry', *Contemporary Review*, vol.18, 1871, pp.334–50.

Burne-Jones, exh. cat., Hayward Gallery, London (Arts Council of Great Britain) 1975.

Georgiana Burne-Jones, *Memorials of Edward Burne-Jones*, London 1904, 2 vols.

Deborah Cherry and Griselda Pollock, 'Woman as Sign in Pre-Raphaelite Literature: A Study of the Representation of Elizabeth Siddall', *Art History*, vol.7, 1984, pp.206–27.

Sidney Colvin, 'Rossetti as a Painter', *Magazine of Art*, vol.6, 1883, pp.177–83.

Walter Crane, *An Artist's Reminiscences*, 2nd ed., London 1907.

Bram Dijkstra, *Idols of Perversity: Fantasies of Feminine Evil in Fin-de-Siècle Culture*, Oxford 1986.

Oswald Doughty, *A Victorian Romantic: Dante Gabriel Rossetti*, 2nd ed., London 1963.

Oswald Doughty and John Robert Wahl (eds.), *Letters of Dante Gabriel Rossetti*, Oxford 1965–8, 4 vols.

Daphne Du Maurier (ed.), *The Young George Du Maurier: Letters 1860–67*, London 1951.

Alicia Craig Faxon, *Dante Gabriel Rossetti*, new ed., London 1994.

Henry James, *The Painter's Eye*, ed. John L. Sweeney, Madison, Wisconsin 1989.

Frederic Leighton, exh. cat., Royal Academy of Arts, London 1996.

Frederick Sandys 1829–1904, exh. cat., Brighton Museum and Art Gallery 1974

Alastair Grieve, *The Art of Dante Gabriel Rossetti*, Norwich 1973–8, 3 parts.

The Grosvenor Gallery, exh. cat., Yale Center for British Art, New Haven 1996.

Martin Harrison and Bill Waters, *Burne-Jones*, 2nd ed., London 1989.

James McNeill Whistler, exh. cat., Tate Gallery, London 1994.

Jeremy Maas, *The Victorian Art World in Photographs*, London 1984.

Linda Merrill, *A Pot of Paint: Aesthetics on Trial in 'Whistler v. Ruskin'*, Washington and London 1992.

F.W.H. Myers, 'Rossetti and the Religion of Beauty', in *Essays Classical and Modern*, London 1883, II, pp. 312–34.

Christopher Newall, *The Grosvenor Gallery Exhibitions*, Cambridge 1995.

Griselda Pollock, 'Woman as Sign: Psychoanalytic Readings', in *Vision and Difference*, London and New York 1988, pp. 120–54.

The Pre-Raphaelites, exh. cat., Tate Gallery, London 1984.

William Michael Rossetti, *Dante Gabriel Rossetti as Designer and Writer*, London 1889.

—(ed.), *Rossetti Papers 1862 to 1870*, London 1903.

John Ruskin, *The Works of John Ruskin*, eds. E.T. Cook and Alexander Wedderburn, London 1903–12, 39 vols.

William Bell Scott, *Autobiographical Notes*, ed. W. Minto, London 1892, 2 vols.

Gayle Marie Seymour, 'The Life and Work of Simeon Solomon (1840–1905)', unpublished Ph.D. thesis, University of California, Santa Barbara 1986.

Robert de la Sizeranne, 'In Memoriam: Sir Edward Burne-Jones, Bart.', *Magazine of Art*, vol. 22, 1898, pp. 513–20.

Alison Smith, *The Victorian Nude*, Manchester 1996.

Sarah Phelps Smith, 'Dante Gabriel Rossetti's Flower Imagery and the Meaning of his Painting', unpublished Ph.D. thesis, University of Pittsburgh 1978.

Solomon: A Family of Painters, exh. cat., Geffrye Museum, London 1985.

F.G. Stephens, 'Dante Gabriel Rossetti', *Portfolio Monograph*, London 1894.

Virginia Surtees, *The Paintings and Drawings of Dante Gabriel Rossetti (1828–1882): A Catalogue Raisonné*, Oxford 1971, 2 vols.

—(ed.), *The Diaries of George Price Boyce*, Norwich 1980.

Algernon Charles Swinburne, 'Simeon Solomon', *Dark Blue*, vol.1, 1871, pp.568–77.

—*William Blake*, London 1868.

—(with William Michael Rossetti) *Notes on the Royal Academy Exhibition, 1868*, London 1868.

M.S. Watts, *George Frederic Watts*, London 1912, 3 vols.

Oscar Wilde, 'The Grosvenor Gallery', *Dublin University Magazine*, vol.90, 1877, pp.118–26.

W.B. Yeats, 'Symbolism in Painting' (1898), repr. in *Essays and Introductions*, London 1961.

Index

Photographic
Credits